Spirituality and Ageing

of related interest

Wholeness in Later Life
Ruth Bright
ISBN 1 85302 447 3

Hearing the Voice of People with Dementia
Opportunities and Obstacles
Malcolm Goldsmith
ISBN 1 85302 406 6

Past Trauma in Later Life
European Perspectives on Therapeutic Work with Older People
Edited by Linda Hunt, Mary Marshall and Cherry Rowlings
ISBN 1 85302 446 5

Dementia
New Skills for Social Workers
Edited by Alan Chapman and Mary Marshall
ISBN 1 85302 257 8

Dementia
Challenges and New Directions
Edited by Susan Hunter
ISBN 1 85302 312 4

Confused Professionals?
The Social Construction of Dementia
Nancy H. Harding and Colin Palfrey
ISBN 1 85302 257 8

Elder Abuse
Best Practice in Britain and Canada
Edited by Jacki Pritchard
ISBN 1 85302 704 9

Drugs and Dementia
A Guide for Carers and Clinicians
Stephen Hopker
ISBN 1 85302 760 X

Spirituality and Ageing

Edited by Albert Jewell

Jessica Kingsley Publishers
London and Philadelphia

First published in the United Kingdom in 1999 by
Jessica Kingsley Publishers Ltd
116 Pentonville Road
London N1 9JB, England
and
325 Chestnut Street
Philadelphia, PA 19106, U S A
www.jkp.com

Second Impression 1999

Copyright © 1999 Jessica Kingsley Publishers
Except Chapter 3 Copyright © 1993 Metropolitan Anthony of Sourozh
Chapter 6 Copyright © 1997 *The Month*
Chapter 7 Copyright © 1993 Spiritual Eldering Institute
Chapter 8 Copyright © 1997 Rabbi Zalman Schachter-Shalomi

Library of Congress Cataloging in Publication Data
A CIP catalogue record for this book is available from the Library of Congress

British Library Cataloguing in Publication Data
Spirituality and ageing
1. Spirituality 2. Spiritual life 3. Aged
I. Jewell, Albert
248.8'5

ISBN 1 85302 631 X

Printed and Bound in Great Britain by
Athenaeum Press, Gateshead, Tyne and Wear

Contents

Acknowledgements

Spirituality in Ageing arose out of the Sir Halley Stewart Project, the purpose of which has been to raise awareness of the spiritual needs of older people and encourage interest in the spirituality of ageing.

Most of the chapters are specially commissioned. However, some first appeared elsewhere and the Editor and Publishers express their thanks to the following:

- The Christian Council on Ageing who first published the contribution by Metropolitan Anthony of Sourozh and an earlier version of the chapter by Lady Helen Oppenheimer
- The Editor of *The Month,* the quarterly journal published by Heythrop College in which the chapter by James A. Crampsey SJ first appeared
- Rabbi Zalman Schachter-Shalomi of the Spiritual Eldering Institute, Naropa Institute, Boulder, Colorado, USA which retains copyright of the chapter written by Dr Jenny Goodman.

Introduction

Albert Jewell

It may legitimately be questioned whether there is a 'spirituality *of* ageing', either in the sense of a universally acceptable spiritual interpretation of the common human experience of growing older, or in the sense of a spirituality that can be specifically associated with ageing persons as distinct from those who are younger. Certainly it should not be held that there is only one kind of spirituality appropriate to old age. 'Spirituality *and* ageing' is therefore a less contentious expression.

Under whichever title there are, however, two important primary questions. The first being, what do we mean by 'ageing'? Who are 'the aged'? A convenient marker may appear to be that of retirement. However, this is a relatively modern concept originating in the western world and has little relevance in many other cultures where elders go on contributing to the economy of the household and community in one way or another until they die. And even in contemporary Britain the age of 'retirement' is becoming much more fluid, although few would wish to argue with the contention that losing a major role in life is of great significance to the individual concerned and those closest to them.

It is becoming customary to refer to the 'third age' and the 'fourth age' of life. The former broadly relates to the seventh and eighth decades of life and the latter to the remainder of one's lifespan. In their sixties and well into their seventies the vast majority of people continue in reasonable health and are able to live full and active lives. In the later stages depletions can multiply and losses increase in regard to roles, bereavements and domicile, all of which have major impact upon what may be termed one's 'personhood', in the sense of identity and self-image. What is certain is that ageing is a process which has cumulative effect at all levels of our being and which leads inexorably towards death.

The other primary question is, what do we mean by 'spirituality'? Definitions abound. One of the shortest, attributed to Robert Warren, is that it comprises 'the recovery of our lost humanity'. In recent years health care NHS trusts have produced guidelines for whole-person care in which spiritual needs are given a due place. The following description of spirituality is favoured by the Brighton and South Downs Trust:

> A quality that goes beyond religious affiliation, that strives for inspiration, reverence, awe, meaning and purpose, even in those who do not believe in any god. The spiritual dimension tries to be in harmony with the universe, strives for answers about the infinite and comes into focus when a person faces emotional stress, physical illness and death'.
> (Murray and Zenter 1986)

If this sounds rather individualistic, the following more succinct and overtly theistic definition of spiritual well-being has been developed by the American National Interfaith Coalition on Ageing: 'the affirmation of life in a relationship with God, self, community and environment that nurtures and celebrates wholeness' (Moberg 1983).

The thrust of the contributions to this volume is broad and wide-ranging. Spirituality has to do with those intangibles that are nonetheless of vital importance to most human beings: values, relationships, and the discovery of meaning and purpose in life. Whether or not they regard themselves as 'religious' in the sense of being identified with a particular religious tradition, denomination or group, most reflective persons recognise that they are spiritual beings whose fulfilment lies beyond the merely material and physical. It will therefore be evident that in this way older people are no different from those in their early or middle years of life. People of all ages share basic human needs that include:

- love (the receiving and giving of affection)
- faith (someone or something to believe in)
- hope (something to look forward to)
- peace (finding a measure of stability and tranquillity)
- worship (a sense of awe and the attribution of value or 'worth' to whomever or whatever is deemed to merit it).

Such values remain basic to all human beings, whether or not they posit any kind of divine being, assume that there is some form of after-life or seek the fulfilment of these needs within a particular religious tradition.

Nevertheless, this shared human spirituality does tend to be focused in specific ways for older people. Part of the reason for this is circumstantial. As already noted, old age does bring its depletions and losses that can cause increased dependency, isolation and depression. In a society that tends to be ageist, marginalising old people and making them feel a burden upon others, the need is great for the affirmation of their continuing value as unique and socially connected human beings and of their wisdom as a resource for others. On the brighter side, advancing age does certainly bring its compensations and joys: the freedom of retirement, significant life events such as major birthdays and anniversaries, grand parenthood and great-grand parenthood, thus giving ample opportunity to express that innate human instinct to celebrate along with other people.

The other reason for the different spiritual focus of advancing years is more existential. In what they might regard as the second half of life people are inevitably rather more aware of the nearer approach of death. Reflective older people can no longer avoid those ultimate questions: What in the end is life all about? Will the world be a better place for my having lived in it? Is there anything beyond? Can there really be a God? Old age is as likely to be a time of deep and serious doubt, even despair, as it is to be one of serene faith and confidence in the face of death. Many older persons, who in their earlier years had a certain and sometimes unquestioning faith, will confess that they now believe far less, or feel that far fewer values are of real and abiding significance for them. However, the wheat having been sifted from the chaff, what remains may assume much greater importance. An aged Bishop Lightfoot last century perhaps speaks for such older people in his reported profession: 'I am content to leave a thousand questions open, providing I am convinced on two or three main lines'.

There are perhaps two ways in particular in which consciously facing death shapes the spirituality of many older people. First, the seeking of reconciliation becomes a very high priority. Older people will frequently confess that their deepest desire is to die at peace: with their fellows, with their god, and therefore with themselves. The damage and hurts we inflict on one another as human beings cry out for resolution even though they may lie buried deep in the psyche. The unfinished business of human relationships from our earlier years becomes the pressing business of our later years. It is tempting for other people to try to paper over the cracks and make out that such things are of little real importance, but to do so is to desecrate what is truly holy ground. The need, before it is too late, to become reconciled with significant others and to find the healing of painful memories is a legitimate and urgent focus of spirituality in ageing. Many would see this as being undergirded by an even more basic need for at-one-ment with God. The approach of death also underlines the search for what may be called 'integrity' or 'integration' – in the sense of wholeness in its spiritual rather than its physical dimension, for the depletions and diminishments of old age are incontrovertible. In our later years, and once again before it is too late, there surfaces the deep desire somehow to pull life together and make sense of the whole. Earlier in our lives we were necessarily preoccupied with the tasks that press upon us at each successive stage: growing up, becoming educated, finding employment, making relationships, getting on in life and, for many though not all, getting married, establishing a home and raising a family. When we are old we have the opportunity at last to reflect upon life as a whole, to make sense of it as best we can, in order (as some would see it) to offer that integrated and completed life back to the life-giver, or at least feel that we will have left the world a slightly better place for our having lived in it. To find some degree of integration, spiritual wholeness, is the consuming desire of many aged people. The approach of death gives the search for reconciliation and integration an almost eschatological resonance.

The production of this book arises from the recognition that in Britain we are an ageing population. We need not rehearse all the demographics here but the proportion of those over 65 seems set to rise from 17 per cent to 26 per cent in the next 35 years and those over 85 almost to double. Much help is available to older people in dealing with their material needs, thanks to organisations like Age Concern and Help the Aged; the University of the Third Age encourages intellectual stimulation and a continuing positive contribution to the community, and there is a wide variety of interest and activity groups to choose from. However, as one retiring cleric put it recently, perhaps somewhat dramatically, 'No one asks you how you are going to prepare to meet your God!'

In fact, spiritual resources are also available, though they may take some seeking out. Most of the major historic religions coming from the Middle or Far East (and many so-called 'primitive' religions) give to older people a respect and honour which is in direct contrast to prevailing western attitudes. The 'wisdom' of old age is regarded as an essential and significant ingredient of society. Within the Christian tradition there are deep spiritual reservoirs within the Roman and Orthodox traditions – rather more, it has to be admitted, than in much of mainstream Protestantism with its almost inevitable 'work/ achievement ethic'. Perhaps most exciting of all, there are those who today are finding a spirituality capable of embracing dementia, a condition in which so much is stripped away from the person that only the essence may seem to remain, if indeed that, and which challenges all our usual notions of personhood. In bringing together such varied approaches to spirituality in ageing, this book is currently unique of its kind, but the hope is that it will not long remain so as interest continues to grow in this vital area.

It is offered to a cross-section of people. To date, little is done in initial or in-service ministerial training to help equip future and present practitioners with an adequate framework of spirituality within which to offer pastoral care to older people. Lay pastoral workers have a similar need. Whereas the spiritual (or at least the religious) dimension has always been acknowledged within hospital-based medical care, the more recently emergent field of social care has tended to adopt a secular model in which spirituality is seen to have little or no place. Now, however, there is an expectation that social workers will assess the spiritual needs (amongst all the other needs) of older people seeking care services. They therefore have a need to know 'where older people are at' in regard to spirituality. Not least, it is hoped that older people themselves will find much encouragement in the pages that follow in attending to the spiritual agenda of their latter days. Ultimately of course this book is for all, because each and every one of us inexorably grows older even as we read. The spirituality of ageing is surely something that everyone needs to address if we would 'restore our lost humanity' or enhance the humanity we have already discovered.

CHAPTER 1

Is there a Spirituality for the Elderly?

An Ignatian Approach

Gerard W. Hughes SJ

The spiritual exercises of St Ignatius Loyola, written in the sixteenth century, are becoming increasingly popular today among Christians of all denominations. I have been asked to write this chapter in answer to the question, 'Have the spiritual exercises anything to offer to the elderly?' The brief answer is, 'Yes, lots, even although Ignatius was a youngster in his late twenties when he began writing them'.

Inigo, as Ignatius was called in his youth, was a Basque nobleman, born in 1493 and brought up in the Spanish court, from which he emerged in his early twenties, vain, arrogant, ambitious, with a streak of Don Quixote in him. In his late twenties he was defending the city of Pamplona against overwhelmingly superior French troops. The city's governor advised surrender, but Inigo insisted in fighting on, until a cannon ball struck him on the knees, severely damaging one and wounding the other. The city surrendered. The French, in those chivalrous days, tended the wounded Inigo as best they could and sent him back to Loyola castle, where he lived. There he lay for months in great pain, waiting for his legs to heal.

Inigo had a great gift of daydreaming, which could occupy him for hours at a time. His first daydreams were about the great deeds he would do once his legs had mended and the great lady whose love he would win. She was, according to a short autobiography which he dictated in his latter years, 'no mere duchess'! However, in spite of the greatness of the lady, he grew tired of his daydreams and asked for novels. Novels were in short supply in those days, and they had none at Loyola: the only books they could give him were a life of Christ and a book of lives of the saints. In his boredom he began reading these. He began daydreaming again, but this time he was dreaming about outdoing the saints, saying to himself, 'If Dominic can do it, so can I. If Francis can do it, so can I'. For weeks he alternated between the two sets of daydreams, of heroic deeds and of the great lady on the one hand, then of outdoing the saints on the other.

Then he noticed something which was to change his life. He noticed a difference in the after-effects of the daydreams. Both were enjoyable at the time, but the first set left him bored, empty and sad, while dreams about outdoing the saints left him hopeful, happy and strengthened. Later, he was to call this discovery his first lesson in 'discerning the spirits', what we might call 'learning to read our moods'. So he decided to become a saint, although he was not too clear as to how. He decided to start with a walk to Jerusalem, where conversion of the Muslim might be a modest start to his saintly career!

He went limping off from Loyola. As pilgrimage was a hazardous undertaking in those days, pilgrims were advised to make a general confession before starting out. Inigo stopped at a place called Montserrat, found a patient Benedictine, and had so much to confess that it took him three days to complete it. He then continued to a place called Manresa, where he stayed for about nine months, undergoing a series of inner experiences of darkness and of light. It was out of this experience that he eventually wrote his book of the Spiritual Exercises.

The Spiritual Exercises are a series of Scripture-based, Christ-centred meditations and contemplations. Ignatius assumed that by making these Exercises, an individual would begin to experience changes of mood and feeling, of happiness, sadness, peace, agitation etc. and by reflecting on these experiences, as he had reflected on the after-effects of his daydreams, individuals would become more aware of their creative and destructive tendencies. By pursuing the creative and avoiding the destructive, they would then discover God's will.

The Spiritual Exercises are primarily designed for those who have to make an important life decision. We tend to think of the elderly as those for whom it is now too late to be making important decisions: we just have to live with the decisions we have made. While it is true that the elderly are not usually concerned with career or state-of-life decisions, they are concerned with an even more fundamental decision: how to face the inevitability of death. This may seem a very morbid prospect: in fact, facing our ageing and the prospect of death can become a life-giving process, for we can then find that our later years are by far the happiest and the most fulfilling.

The American philosopher Thoreau once wrote, 'Most people live lives of quiet desperation'. There is so much truth in that comment! In youth, most of us are full of dreams, hopes and ambitions. We set our hearts on fulfilling these dreams, but relentless reality keeps frustrating us. Even if we do succeed in fulfilling some of them, becoming wealthy or successful, we may find that we have worn ourselves out, damaged others and lost our friends and family in the process, and the success turns to ashes in our mouths. With failing physical strength, we no longer have the energy or ability to pursue what once gave us life, and we are left to contemplate our own emptiness. Even if we have been religiously committed people, we may find that in old age we are assailed by doubts about faith, and that God disappears as our physical energy abates.

In his Preface to the Spiritual Exercises, which is a skeletal summary of the whole book, Ignatius opens with the sentence, 'We are created to praise, reverence and serve God, and by this means to save our souls', a very traditional Christian formulation of the purpose of human life. The next sentence is, 'Everything on the face of the earth is created to help us to do this'. The extraordinariness of this last sentence can easily escape us. 'Everything' includes failing strength of body and mind, disappointment, disillusion, failure, guilt, feelings of helplessness and hopelessness. His spirituality has been described as 'Finding God in all things', including old age!

Francis Thompson described God as the Hound of Heaven, who pursues us down the arches of the years until he corners us and declares: 'Ah, fondest, blindest, weakest, I am He whom thou seekest'.

St Augustine, looking back on his life, wrote, 'God, you created me for yourself, and my soul is restless until it rest in You'. Much of the pain we experience in life is the pain of our own ego. We pour our energies into building up our own ego-kingdom, its foundations our own sense of self-importance, its ramparts our wealth, status and achievements, expecting the rest of creation to praise, reverence and serve us. Creation does not comply, at least not for long, and our kingdom crumbles. This feels like disaster. If we can face the disaster, it can turn out to be the greatest blessing, for it can free us from the prison of our narrow ego-centred hopes and ambitions, and open us up to the wonders of creation, God's sacrament, and to the joy that it brings.

In old age we can begin to feel useless, for we are no longer capable of doing what is called 'a proper day's work'. This can become a blessing, not a curse. The Psalmist says, 'Be still and know that I am God'. In old age, nature helps us to be more still, and in the stillness we can better listen to God, our teacher.

The prophet Isaiah says:

When the Lord has given you the bread of suffering and the water of distress, he who is your teacher will hide no longer, and you will see your teacher with your own eyes. Whether you turn to right or to left, your ears will hear these words behind you, 'This is the way, follow it.' (Isaiah 30: 20–22)

So how do we listen to God? By being still and letting God pray in us. Prayer has been described as 'raising the mind and heart to God'. All prayer should lead us eventually into stillness, and in the stillness we can begin to become aware of the truth. The truth is that we cannot pray: it is the Spirit of God who prays within us. Too much effort on our part, too much thought, and above all too much moralising, can deafen us to God praying within us.

Here are some very simple ways of praying, and our prayer can never be too simple. Jesus said, 'Unless you become as little children, you cannot enter the kingdom of heaven'.

Sit, and be as relaxed as possible. To have our backs reasonably straight, but not rigid, helps to keep us awake and attentive. Listen to God call you by your name and say to you, 'Don't be afraid, for I am with you'. Your mind may come up with all kinds of objections: 'How do I know there is a God?' or 'How do I know this will do me any good?' or memories, whether good or bad, may come unbidden. Acknowledge your thoughts, questions and memories, but do not tangle with them: just let them pass through your mind and keep your attention on God's word being spoken to you. You are letting God be the God of love and compassion to you. There is nothing more profitable we can do in life. It sounds excessively simple. That is why we find it so difficult: we love complications!

If you just read this chapter, you will probably have forgotten it by tomorrow. But if you keep doing this simple exercise, your whole life will change, for you are letting God in, and everything will begin to seem different. The Psalmist recommends this exercise:

> Yahweh, my heart has no lofty ambitions, my eyes do not look too high. I am not concerned with great affairs, or marvels beyond my scope. Enough for me to keep my soul tranquil and quiet, like a child in its mother's arms, as content as a child that has been fed. Israel, rely on Yahweh, now and always. (Psalm 131)

In old age, memories of childhood and of youth often keep recurring, sometimes happy memories, sometimes sad. If they keep recurring, it is good to dwell on them, if you can, for God is in all things. Look at the happy memories first, relish them, and thank God for them. Everything is God's gift, a sign of God's love and a token of God's wanting to share His life with you, not because you have been good and virtuous, or have achieved great things, but because you are you. With the painful memories, do not do violence to yourself by forcing yourself to look at them, but if you can, present them to God. If they are hurtful memories of conflict, whether you did the damage, or the damage was done to you, imagine the scene again, but with Christ present in it. Tell Him of your pain and hurt at the injustice done to you by others. Then, in imagination, let those who did the damage speak. Then pray to God to give you His Spirit of forgiveness, and pray for those who have hurt you, whether they are living or dead. If you did the damage, then in imagination beg forgiveness from your victims, pray for them, whether they are living or dead. God is the God of reconciliation, and God is always in the now. This exercise can cleanse our memories and leave us feeling lighter and more at peace. Hurtful memories can return, and we may have to repeat the exercise many times. When Peter asked Jesus, 'How often must I forgive my brother, as many as seven times?' Jesus replied, 'Not seven times I tell you, but seventy times seven'. The offence may have happened only once, but we may have to forgive seventy times seven times. Always keep the focus of your attention on God's goodness rather than on your hurt or your sinfulness, for God is always greater.

Recalling each day's memories is a very useful form of daily prayer. Before going to sleep recall, first of all, the things you have enjoyed during the day. God is the author of all good gifts, so having recalled and relished them, thank God for them, for He has sent you these things with love. In doing this avoid, like the plague, any self-judgement, whether approval or disapproval.

Then ask God to enlighten you so that you can recognise His action more clearly. Look at your moods and feelings during the day, again without any self-judgement. Our moods and feelings normally arise out of our desires. When our desires are satisfied, our mood is good: when our desires are frustrated, then we grow grumpy and take it out on those around us. So ask God to show you the desires underlying your moods and feelings. Then ask yourself, 'On whose kingdom are my desires centred – on my kingdom, or God's?' If they are centred on God's kingdom, then thank Him for that: if they are centred on your kingdom, then beg God to switch the direction of your desires, from ministering to our ego to a longing for His kingdom of truth, of love and of peace.

Sitting and gazing at things without a thought in your head is a very good form of prayer. It might be a tree, a leaf, a flower, a cat or a dog. Use your senses on whatever you are gazing at, touching, scenting, hearing. It is amazing how things can come to life when we do this. God is in everything. Every bush is burning, if only we have the eyes to see. And God is saying to you through all these things, 'Ah, fondest, blindest, weakest, I am He whom thou seekest'. This knowledge is more precious than anything we can ever achieve. And in this knowledge you will find yourself praying for others, your own friends and family, and also for people you have never met, and you will feel great love for them and a longing for their happiness.

Old age can be the happiest, most useful and most fulfilling period of our lives, provided we can let God take over, 'For his Power working us can do infinitely more than we can think or imagine' (Ephesians 3:20).

CHAPTER 2

To Live is to Change

Jeffrey W. Harris

One of the few pieces of Shakespeare which most people know is his description of 'The Seven Ages of Man'. It reads: 'All the world's a stage, and all the men and women merely players: they have their exits and their entrances; and one man in his time plays many parts, his acts being seven ages' (*As You Like It,* Act II).

He then proceeds to describe the seven ages, from infancy to old age. A person in the sixth age is lean, with spectacles on his nose, wearing old clothes now too large, piping and whistling through his few teeth as he speaks in a childish treble. The seventh age is even worse – second childhood, with no teeth, no taste, unable to see and devoid of all quality. Neither picture is attractive!

Life of course cannot be compared to an actor playing a succession of parts. Life is real. Life is the person which is me or you living at a particular time, in particular places, amongst other particular people. We are influenced by all that we experience. Something happens to us and in a moment the direction of our life is changed. For example, we talk of 'falling in love at first sight', meaning that, in a moment, a person's life takes on a new direction and purpose.

It is impossible to say what any person is really like. We so quickly change. One moment we are on top of the world, the next we are in distress. The difference is caused by something we have just experienced. Some changes occur simply because of the passage of time. Older people look back over the course of their lives and wonder if they can see some kind of pattern to it. Was it all worthwhile? Does it all make sense?

When looking for a pattern in life, however, we should never believe that the second part of life is always one of loss and decline.

The Model of Loss and Decline

This model regards the earlier part of our life as a time of progressive growth and development, reaching its peak when we are in our early twenties. For the next thirty years or so, we use what we have learned, but don't attempt significantly to increase our knowledge or change the course we have chosen. At about the age of fifty our powers begin a process of decline which accelerates in our mid-sixties. Things then begin to go wrong with us 'due to our age'. So we regress to a general loss of ability to control our lives.

Many serious questions must be asked about this model. It is not true that we cannot learn new things after we are thirty. We can still learn in our eighties and nineties though the pace of learning is slower. If they are to keep economically active in today's world, many people will need to change their career in their forties and fifties. Those who try, find they *can* learn new disciplines. Many people at retirement begin to study at an advanced level subjects which have long interested them. They cope perfectly well. Those who do not take medical problems seriously and say they are simply due to old age fail to keep the level of health and fitness which they should enjoy. Doing things more slowly is not the same as accepting decline. What is required is an adjustment to our level of expectation.

Those who see life in terms of this model simply react to it. They assume that at a certain age they are too old to learn new things, try new activities, find new interests. Those who deal with older people may also try to fit them into this kind of mould. For example, clergy may think their role is to comfort and console older people rather than to encourage them to face new questions and challenges. Older people need stimulating to approach changes in life positively, believing the best is yet to be.

Yielding Place to New

A much better model to use begins with accepting that to live is to change. As the years pass, we move on from one stage to the next. Given the choice, we might opt to stay as we are, but this is not possible. Moving to the next stage always involves regrets and the loss of things we have enjoyed. But awaiting us are new experiences and the chance to make new friends. The new stage really is much better than we imagined! The positive way to approach life is to be willing to yield the things we enjoy at present and move on to the next stage with hope. Some examples from the life experience of most people will illustrate the point.

Before the moment of our birth, we lived in security, warmed and nourished by our mothers. Probably our first cries were of protest at leaving that world behind. But waiting to receive us in the world with love and affection were almost certainly parents and grandparents, ready to give us security and care. It was a new part of life.

When the time came for us to leave the security of home to make our first venture to primary school, playgroup or nursery school, and learn to mix with others and begin the process of education, we were not very keen to go. That first day was so difficult, but we soon began to enjoy the challenges and the friendships and the skills and knowledge we began to acquire.

In a similar way, when we left school to go on to higher education or to enter the world of work, we lost many friends and the privileges of being at the top of the school. But this was a new phase in life, moving on to take an adult, independent place in the world. There were new challenges and new adventures.

It was the same for most of us when we fell in love and wanted to begin a home of our own, when we had to move to a new town for reasons of employment, when our own family came along, when they grew up and left home. So too eventually when we had to face retirement. Of course, once again we knew we would miss friends and colleagues, and the part we played in a team. But we now had a new freedom to do the things we never had time for before, to visit friends and places, make new friends, take up new challenges of voluntary service. Yielding place to the new was not all loss, though inevitably there were some regrets. But every new stage brought its opportunities and challenges. We did not need to be afraid!

The Later Stages

Inevitably, as we age, we have fewer things to which we can look forward in this life. The compensation is that we have many things to recall, many precious experiences to relive. We have been to places, done things, made friends, have a host of memories. And if we are fortunate, we have children and grandchildren whom we see. And however old we are, there will be more to come.

Part of the ground for hope of life in a world to come lies in the experiences we have had in this life. We could never know what the next stage would be like until we let go of the past and embraced the new. And when we embraced the new, we knew then we had no reason to fear. There is no reason to believe that this pattern will be different when life on this earth comes to its natural end.

The concept of a life beyond death raises questions about our spiritual nature. In his study of the psychologist Jung, Anthony Storr (1986) has a chapter called 'The process of individuation'. He calls this the central concept of Jung's psychology. It is the process of bringing together the conflicting sides of our nature so that we find a sense of unity, purpose, peace. It is essentially a process which takes place in the second half of life. Jung thought that the first half of our life was rather one-sided. We are so busy with practical things that we have no time to devote to the cultivation of our inner lives. His experience of patients in the second part of their lives led him to regard this time as a 'spiritual quest or journey'.

The Spiritual Quest

The words 'spiritual' and 'spirituality' are in fairly common use today, but people use them to convey different ideas. It is important to try to explain what is meant by them.

There are certain qualities which appear to distinguish a human being from the rest of creation. It is true that, looked at from one perspective, we are the product of the natural evolutionary processes of creation. However, there are also things which make us different from every other creature. One major factor is the level of human intelligence. What makes us unique, however, is our spiritual nature. This can be explored under three headings.

The Potential and Significance of each Individual

When we hold a newly born baby in our arms, we feel a sense of awe and wonder at this fragile gift of human life, totally dependent on others for everything. But there are latent talents and skills in this new life. Growth and development are needed, physically, mentally, emotionally and spiritually, so that in time there may be a complete person, fulfilling all the potential which there is at our birth, and able to take our proper place in the world. It is important that in addition to a healthy body, educated mind and warm emotions, we learn to love and be loved, to appreciate beauty, truth, music and literature. We need to develop a sense of wonder and awe at the created universe of which we are part. These are spiritual values. They can lead to a deeper sense of the life of the spirit and to a relationship with God.

Of course, we do not all start equal. Some are stronger or cleverer than others. Some begin from a position of considerable disadvantage. Others have special problems which are difficult to overcome. We have to try to make the best of what we have and are. Moreover, everyone has weaknesses and failures and is aware they have acted wrongly at certain times. They made decisions which have harmed others. Unless we can find forgiveness for them, we have to learn to live with the consequences. Our moral nature, and our need of forgiveness and renewal belong to the spiritual side of our lives.

The essential element in our humanity, however, is that all of us need to find our place in the human family. John Donne reminds us that 'No man is an Island, entire of it self'. From our earliest years, we have to develop relationships with others, starting with our families. They are fostered by friendship, education, sport, leisure activities and employment. In various ways, we make our contribution to the well-being of society.

We need to be aware particularly of those who are disadvantaged. Our own personal happiness must not be the sole or even main object of living. We need to have regard to the wider world and to learn to love our neighbour as ourselves.

The reason why we must learn to be sensitive to the needs of others is that each one of us is of significance and entitled to be treated with dignity and respect. When our spiritual sense is undeveloped, we are likely to treat others with indifference, prejudice, cruelty and even exploitation. Our concern is primarily for personal satisfaction.

So 'spiritual' and 'spirituality' concern us all, whatever our gender, family background or race. And we all have to continue the process of development throughout the whole of our lives, seeking as we do so to contribute to the emergence of a community and world in which there is justice for all and in which all are able to live at peace with others. Only then can we hope that we may find a sense of wholeness and be at peace with ourselves.

The Search for Meaning and Purpose

Deep down within them, most people feel that both creation and life have meaning and purpose. We live in a material world, and we are born through a physical process. But this world seems to operate in an intelligent, predictable way. It is this fact that makes scientific thinking possible. By using human reason, we can find out what some of these processes are. And it leads to the questions: how did it all begin, and why? What is its meaning and purpose?

Some thinkers today have concluded that there is nothing real except the physical universe. Ultimately the pattern of our life is controlled by our 'selfish genes'. Life has no ultimate meaning. The best that we can do is to act with courage and integrity, and work with others to make a better world. However, most feel instinctively that there is more to life than that.

In a recent book called *The Mind of God* (1992), Paul Davies, Professor of Mathematical Physics, concluded:

> We who are children of the universe – animated stardust – can never-theless reflect on the nature of that same universe, even to the extent of glimpsing the rules on which it runs… What does it mean?… I cannot believe that our existence in this universe is a mere quirk of fate, an accident of history, an incidental blip in the great cosmic drama… Through conscious beings, the universe has generated self-awareness. We are truly meant to be here. (p.232)

Somewhere, in our universe, there is meaning and purpose. This raises huge questions. Is there indeed more to life than our span of years here on earth? Do those things for which we search and for which we sacrifice have lasting significance? In his book, *Science and Christian Belief* (1994), Dr John Polkinghorne, until recently Master of a Cambridge college, and both scientist and theologian, says:

> It seems to me that many educated people in the Western world view religious belief with a certain wistful wariness. They would like some sort of faith, but feel that it is only to be had on terms which amount to intellectual suicide. They can neither accept the idea of God nor quite leave it alone. I want to try to show that although faith goes beyond what is logically demonstrable … it is capable of rational motivation. (p.57)

He goes on to show that there are very good reasons for believing life does have meaning and purpose. Those who live their lives with this belief are engaged upon an important spiritual quest.

The Religious Dimension

Trying to think deeply about the meaning and purpose of life is to engage in a religious quest. E.S.Waterhouse (1947) defined religion as 'man's attempt to supplement his felt insufficiency by allying himself with a higher order of being which he believes is manifest in the world and can be brought into sympathetic relationship with himself, if rightly approached'. This is of course a general definition. Different people make the attempt in different ways.

In his book *Does God Exist?* (1980) Hans Kung has a chapter with an interesting title, 'The Many Names of the One God'. He writes:

> Not only Muslims in Allah, but also Hindus in Brahma, Buddhists in the Absolute, Chinese in heaven or in the Tao are seeking one and the same absolutely first, absolutely last reality, which for Jews and Christians is the one true God. (p.627)

Within Britain, the various world religions are practised, but the basis of our national life lies in the Christian religion. At its centre is the belief that God is our Father (though the word expresses God's concern for all His children, and should not be taken to mean that God is male). Also, God is good, God loves each person and is never indifferent to their needs. God is One who wishes to save or liberate His people from everything which oppresses them. At the centre of His Kingdom or Rule, is justice (or 'righteousness'). These are values we learn most of all through Jesus Christ. If they are true, then they have important consequences for each of us.

The Encounter with God

The Bible is recognised by Christians in all branches of the Church as the sacred book which records the foundations of their faith. The Old Testament describes the Covenant relationship between God and the Jewish people. The New Testament describes a new Covenant relationship between God and people of all nations and kinds, made possible through Jesus Christ. The golden thread which runs through the whole of the Bible is the record of the human experience of God.

We learn that it is always God who takes the initiative to make Himself known to human beings. (Theologians call this 'grace'.) However long they search, people will never find God unless God reveals Himself to them. God is the God of Abraham, Isaac and Jacob, the One who calls Moses at the site of the burning bush in Sinai, and sends him to bring about the liberation of the Hebrews from the oppression of Pharaoh. And the record continues for many centuries in which the Hebrews developed their understanding of God's nature and purpose.

The New Testament begins with the coming of Jesus and goes on to tell of His ministry, teaching, sufferings, death, resurrection and ascension. And then comes the gift of the Holy Spirit and the founding of the Church. But always God takes the initiative to make Himself known. The supreme unveiling of God's nature and purpose is in Jesus.

There are certainly dark pages in the two thousand years of the history of the Church, but in every age God has made Himself known to men and women of all kinds, and called them to witness and to serve in ways that make life in this world what God wants it to be.

This shows that if we wish to find the way to God, we should not begin by trying to sort out our ideas about religion, or about God and His world. At the centre of our lives is a capacity to open ourselves to others, to form relationships of love and trust. When we open our lives to God, reach out and ask Him to come to us, we discover the reality of His Presence. The New Testament word for this reaching out is 'faith'.

Blaise Pascal, a Frenchman who lived in the seventeenth century, has had a great influence on all the great thinkers who have come after him, right up to the present time. He was a genius in mathematics, physics and engineering. The greatest moment of his life took place in 'the year of grace 1654, on Monday, 23rd November, from about half past ten in the evening until half past midnight' (Pascal 1966). It was an experience of supreme ecstasy through which he came to know the certainty of God. His great phrase is 'God of Abraham, God of Isaac, God of Jacob, not of philosophers and scholars'. Pascal found that a person only apprehends God with the heart, and not with reason. He wrote the well-known line, 'The heart has its reasons of which reason knows nothing; we know this in countless ways'.

Pascal had discovered what others had found through the centuries. We do not encounter God by engaging in an intellectual search. He is found in experience, as we let our heart reach out for Him. God comes to us, and we discover who He is. Pascal added to the quotation above: 'God of Jesus Christ. He can only be found in the ways taught in the Gospel. He can only be kept by the ways taught in the Gospel.' Through his experience, Pascal spoke of God as the absolute ground of certainty.

Can We Ever Be Certain?

There are many Christians who are ready to say 'I know'. At the end of Hans Kung's book *Does God Exist?* he writes:

> Despite all upheavals and doubts for man today, the only appropriate answer must be that with which believers of all generations from ancient times have again and again professed their faith. It begins with faith, You

God we praise, and ends in trust, In You have I hoped. I shall never be put to shame. (Kung 1980, p.702)

They are words of a personal relationship. None of us can prove by logical argument the reality of our love for someone. Yet in our hearts we know that it is real.

The sociologist Peter Berger, in his book *A Rumour of Angels* (1969), helps us with what he calls 'signals of transcendence'. By this phrase, he means that there are things we experience in this life which appear to point to ultimate realities beyond this world.

An example is that of a child waking in the night. He is alone in the darkness and feels afraid. He cries out for his mother, the only person who can bring him a sense of peace and trust. She turns on the lamp, and says to her child, 'Don't be afraid, everything is all right'. Usually, reassured, the child returns to sleep.

Berger points out that the mother is not lying to the child, because her reassurance is based on a belief about reality as such. She is saying, 'In this world, everything is in order, everything is all right'. We really can trust this.

Another example is that of children playing hopscotch in the park. They are completely intent on their game, closed to the world outside it, happy in their concentration. Time has stood still for them. The outside world has for the duration of the game ceased to exist. And by implication, pain and death, which are the law of that world, have ceased to exist.

Adults listening to some great music or feeling 'out of this world' in the company of one they love dearly also know that they have lost all sense of time. Those experiences truly point us to what is meant by 'eternity'. Berger gives us other illustrations. They are all signals of a transcendent reality – of God.

As we move through the third and fourth ages of life, and are conscious of our ageing and the loss of loved ones through death, most of us ask, 'Can we know? Can we be sure?' Pascal, the genius mentioned above, wrote some words in his *Pensées* which may be helpful: 'Either God exists or he does not … Reason can decide nothing … What will you bet? … If you win, you win everything. If you lose, you lose nothing. Bet then that he exists, without hesitating.' This faith that God exists can help us find peace and strength in the later years of our lives – even at the last.

When Sir Malcolm Sargent, remembered most for conducting many Promenade Concerts, was dying of cancer in 1967, Donald Coggan, then Archbishop of York, visited him. He has made known Sargent's deathbed words: 'I always had faith. Now I have *knowledge*' (Reid 1968, p.4). Finding this peace and knowledge is a journey of the spirit – a pilgrimage. It gives a conviction of meaning and purpose to life which carries us through the ultimate change into the world of eternity. To discover its reality is one of the greatest possibilities open to ageing people.

CHAPTER 3

The Spirituality of Old Age

Metropolitan Anthony of Sourozh

I write not from an objective point of view but just as an old man, now in my eighties, and from the experience I have gained both as a physician and as a priest within the last 50 years. The problems of the old can be centred on the past, the present and the future. One of the things that an old or ageing person has to face is his own past. It applies to people and it applies to nations. I think it was Solzhenitsyn who said that a nation which has not come to terms with its past cannot resolve any problems with its future. This applies to us all; as long as we turn away from our past, close our eyes, do not want to remember, we cannot resolve problems in the present or the future.

The Past

So the first thing an old person must do is determine not to escape his or her own past; to be ready, when the past emerges in memories or on the reappearance of some long forgotten person, to look squarely at any unresolved problem. I would like simply to single out two examples.

A number of years ago one of the older members of our congregation came to see me and said:

> I don't know what to do. I can't sleep during the night. Thoughts come and go. Images of the past come. Memories come. I have asked the doctor to help me and he has given me sleeping pills but they don't prevent me from having to face these things because then, instead of them being memories and thoughts, they become nightmares, and I can do nothing about it.

I suggested to her something which I later began to believe in even more firmly myself: that it is given to us to live and relive our past until we have solved the problems which emerge. As long as we have not faced a situation in the past, whenever we have not answered a question, it will persist as memory, nightmare or reminiscence. So I suggested to this lady that it is a gift of God that she is so deeply disturbed by events of her own past, because if she were to enter into eternity with all these problems unresolved she would still have to resolve them, but no longer in a situation which lends itself to it. She asked me what to do and I suggested that when a situation emerged she should place herself back in it and relive it, but relive it in the light of all her subsequent experience. Then ask herself: 'All right, God has forced me back into this situation. Would I have acted or spoken the way I did 40, 50 or 70 years ago?'

As long as she could say with all her being, with her fear, with all the experience of her life and her gradually acquired maturity, 'No, if I were again in those circumstances, I would not have done it and I can wholeheartedly renounce it,' then she has died to it.

This notion, this sense of dying to one's past in one way or another, is something very real. I remember someone coming to a priest and saying, 'I have a problem. A number of years ago I did wrong in such a way but though I can state my sin or misdeed I cannot repent. This is not because I am insensitive but because I have an absolutely clear feeling that the person who did it, 20 or 25 years ago, is no longer me. I am no longer that person and I can no longer actively repent of those actions because I am not he who committed them.' This is a point I was making to that old lady. It is given to us to live and relive, to be forced back into all situations of our past which were wrong, painful or distorted, so that from the new maturity we possess we can undo them, resolve them as one can undo a knot and let things go.

The second example is of a similar type but one which resolves itself in a different way. A man in his middle eighties came to see me and asked for advice. When he was a young man of 20 or so he had been an officer in the White Army during the Civil War in Russia. He was deeply in love with a nurse of their unit and she was deeply in love with him. They intended to marry. All was hope and joy but during one of the battles he moved at the wrong moment and shot her dead. He could never, never come to terms with this. He said to me, 'I killed the girl I love. I killed the girl who loved me. I cut short a life that was just blossoming and was all possibility, all future. What can I do?'

I said, 'What have you been doing so far, because this was 60 years back?' He said, 'I have followed the advice of everyone who was prepared to give advice. I prayed for forgiveness, but never felt peace in my heart. I went to confession, wept over my action, received absolution but nothing happened.

I did all the good I could in her name and nothing happened to me inwardly in my heart. I received Communion, I did everything which pious people, clergy or friends suggested.'

And then you know, I thought my heavenly patron must be Baalam's Ass, who brayed out something useful when Baalam the Prophet didn't see the angel standing in front of him. So I listened to Baalam's Ass and advised the man thus: 'Look, you have been asking a priest whom you did not kill, to forgive you. Have you ever asked the girl whom you did kill, to forgive you?'

'She is dead,' he said. 'Yes,' I replied, 'she is dead in the sense that physically her life was cut short by the bullet. But do you believe that God is the God of the living and not the God of the dead?' He said, 'Yes'. 'Well,' I said, 'then she is alive. So when you have read Evening Prayers, settle down in your armchair and talk to her. Ask the Lord to make it possible for her to perceive what you have to say. Tell her of your broken-heartedness, of all you have experienced, of your pain and despair and ask her to forgive you and to pray to the Lord that if she can forgive you wholeheartedly God will bring His peace into your heart.' And all this did happen!

So this is another way of solving a problem if we do believe that God is the God of the living and that everyone is alive for Him. It is not always possible to resolve a situation oneself because others are involved. It is not simply to say, 'I have come to terms with the wrong I did to others'. But one can come to terms with the things that happened. I will come to another aspect of that in a moment.

The past is with us in two ways. Either it is events which have occurred, but have then withered and gone, that have fashioned us; or the past remains in us as unresolved problems, and it is then we must remember that God gives us a chance. Forced back in dreams, in nightmares, in reminiscences, in different encounters, or horrified perhaps by a novel which suddenly depicts our own situation, we must not turn away. We must face it and say, 'If I am the person who did it, it's not the past, it is my present and it must be resolved one way or another'. So much for the problem of the past.

The Present

Now we have come to the problem of the present. When we become old enough to have shed all that was our younger years, certain problems appear. However, there is an intermediate moment, a period during which our mature years are very close to us and yet we feel that they are going away from us. Our physical strength lessens, our mental energies are no longer the same.

Very often, ageing people cling desperately to what is going away and to what they cannot possibly retain.

However we strain our physical energies we cannot be at 70 what we were at 30 and 40. However much we train our mind there are things which we could do with our minds when we were 25 and cannot do when we are 80. So what are we to do? Most people occasionally try to revive the embers, to stir at least a flame, to be for just a moment what they once were. I think this is a mistake, because the more we poke embers the more we reduce them into cinders. The solution which I think right is given to us in a few very beautiful lines by the French writer Victor Hugo:

> The old person who is returning to the primordial source of life is moving out of fleeting time and entering into eternity. One can see fire in the eyes of the young, but one can see light in the eyes of the old! We must realise that there is a time to be a flame but there is also a time to be a light! To be a light, a gentle, peaceful, steady light that shines in the darkness, may be useful, more precious to those people who surround us than if we remain a scorching flame.

Nietzsche, in one of his religious poems, says, 'I am a flame. Whatever I leave becomes ashes.' Well, the danger for an older person is to touch things and reduce them to ashes because he or she can no longer sustain the glowing flame, can only burn and not keep alive the flame. So there is a readjustment which is extremely important: to learn to accept that there can no longer be a burning flame, but there can be a gentle light. We can radiate serenity, peace, reconciliation, instead of a stirring energy that forces people into action. This is a process which each of us must accept, but we cannot be forced into it. If we insist on being flame, sooner or later we will become extinct. Then it will be too late to transform fire into light.

There are so many things one cannot do as one ages and particularly one feels that one is no longer determining events. There is a difference between being passive and being contemplative. What frightens the older person is that the moment comes when he or she cannot determine events: then it means being passive and receiving the blows the events deal. We need to learn to be contemplative, and look at events steadily with all the experience of life, with all the detachment which can be possessed only when we do not rush into action – and only then to speak a word that comes from the depths of serenity, or if you prefer, inner silence. This will be the only word which will be a word of truth because it will give shape to what is within the silence beyond the words.

There are things, however, which people of all ages can do. You do not need to be an old person! Every person who is ageing or who is old can settle down and ask: 'What can I do, what is within my capabilities, my health, my strength, my sight, my hearing, my understanding?' At times one can well help an older person discover something very important, that this person *is* – even if unable to do what he or she could do in the past.

I will give you an example. My grandmother died when she was 95 and at that age she could not do what she had done so well when she was a young woman. One day she insisted on washing-up after lunch. At the end I heard a terrible crash. She walked into my room and said, 'I have broken all the crockery. I had washed it clean and then pushed it with my elbow and there is nothing left of it. Why does God allow me to live now that I am good for nothing – not even capable of washing-up?'

I answered, 'I can give you two reasons for it'. She pricked up her ears, because two reasons seemed a lot. 'Well!' I said, 'The first reason I can give is this. Heaven is full of old ladies. Do you think He can afford to have one more?'. Looking rather affronted, she said: 'No, you are not being serious. I am speaking of something which is very grave.'

I went on, 'Yes, I have a second reason. There is something which, since the world began and until the last judgement and beyond, no one else but you has been able to do.' She looked at me with interest and asked, 'What's that?' I said, 'Since the world began and until eternity unfolds before us, no one else was capable of being my grandmother'.

Now being my grandmother does not simply mean giving birth to my mother and eventually my mother to me. It means a whole situation, a whole relationship. And you know, that made sense to her. So anyone talking with old people who feel they have become useless could say to them: 'No, there is one thing you can do as nobody else can. You are my mother, my grandmother, you are my friend.' Make sure they understand that this is an absolute and abides in definitive, eternal value. It can give such a boost of hope and joy to the person.

Now there is another thing which belongs to the present. It is a fact that as we grow old we may well become dependent because we see badly or because we lose our mind or because we are physically handicapped or because we are seriously ill. And so often old people say: 'Why don't I die? I don't want to be a burden to others!'

That is something we should never allow to be passed unanswered because it signifies hopelessness. If you believe you are just a burden, there is nothing else for you to do other than to kill yourself or let yourself die. But you are never a burden *if* (and there are two 'ifs'). *If* people love you, you are not a burden. They have the joy and privilege of looking with tenderness, concern and intelligence at someone whom they have loved all their lives; and though the word is perhaps ugly, the opportunity to repay all that this person has done. A mother has looked after her children for years, now it is the privilege of the children to look after their mother. But not unconditionally; and this is the second 'if'!

If you are an elderly person who has become dependent on the tenderness, the love and faithfulness of those around you, you must make it easy and possible for them. You must learn to accept what you are given graciously and to make of the relationship of giving and taking a feast and not a calamity for both of you. And you know, to be able to receive graciously, gratefully, joyfully is an art which we do not always possess. Even in short illnesses people are not always capable of doing it, but in longer periods, like ageing, it must be learned and learned soon. We must know that this happens and to be at the receiving end can be a devastating thing or an immensely rewarding one. One of the Psalms says, 'How shall I repay the Lord for all his benefits?' And the answer is, 'I shall accept the cup of salvation and sing His praises unto His cause'.

To accept the gift with joy, with open-heartedness, with shining eyes, giving tenderness in response to tenderness, is not only the best, but the only way of making the giving as easy as possible. On the contrary, when we receive with a cramped heart it says: 'I would fain receive nothing from you, but I am a victim of my rheumatism or my illness or my age, so I must depend on you!' Thus we can transform a love relationship into something which is full of bitterness. It is a schooling we must give to other people when they are ageing, and a school we must go through ourselves as soon as possible, because we all depend on one another's love, whether we are children, grown-up people, married, single or old.

We must learn at all ages how to receive with gratitude, to receive with grace, to receive in such a way that the giving should be a joy for the giver and add new depth to the relationship.

The Future

One more thing to remember. An old person habitually looks to his or her death, and death appears at certain moments as liberation, at other moments as terror. Death appears as liberation when it is not upon us; when death is far enough away we speak of it in these terms. When it is very close, when we feel death within our limbs, we may be afraid of it. And so it is very important to start growing into an attitude to death which is healthy, not waiting until we are already afraid of it but learning long before, as children, as young people, as adults, to look at death in a creative way.

The first thing I think important is to distinguish between the process of dying and death itself, because a number of people would not be afraid of death if they were not afraid of what they had seen of dying and the suffering which accompanies certain illness. This is a different thing from death and in the present state of medicine this has become much less of a problem than it was.

Cicely Saunders, who was one of the best specialists on the problem of dying, said to me that there is no reason nowadays why a patient ill with cancer should either suffer or become over-sedated. There are drugs which, if used skilfully, can prevent this. So one can tell most people that dying will not be a horror. On the other hand, we should never speak as though we could prepare anyone for their death. The trouble is we cannot prepare anyone for anything we have not experienced ourselves, and when people, particularly young clergy, say to a dying person, 'Oh it is all right, you will see how wonderful it is,' this is far from being convincing.

But what can we do about it? We can do several things but one which is absolutely essential is this: we can prepare the person, not to die but to live in eternity. It is only the extent to which a person now in the flesh begins to have an experience of eternal life, that the physical death which will separate soul from body can be faced with equanimity and with hope. St Paul could speak of it when he said: 'For me to die is not to divest myself of temporary life but to clothe myself with eternity.' So that the whole pastoral approach to a dying person is gradually to help them to enter things eternal.

I end with giving you an example which impressed me very much. In the early days when I was a priest in London, I had a friend, older than me, who had had a most difficult life. At 19 he had been taken into a Soviet concentration camp, had gangrene, had his leg amputated at the hip and was then thrown out because he was useless.

He had enough to face, but he fell ill with jaundice and went to hospital where the doctors attending him discovered he had inoperable cancer that filled his stomach and had gone to his liver. He was not told anything about it, but his sister and I were told and I went to see him. He was lying in bed, a strong, tall, handsome man. He said, 'What a bother! I have so much to do in life, and look, I am in bed, they can't even tell me when I will get out of it.' I said, 'Did you not tell me more than once that you longed to stop time, so that you would not have to keep on doing and doing but could simply be. You have never done that, have you?' He said, 'No'. 'Well, God has done it for you. You can do nothing. Learn to be.'

So he looked at me and said, 'Yes, that's true, but how does one do that, because to be means to be in eternity somehow? One cannot just be in thin air, suspended between heaven and earth.' I replied, very simply, 'You must first of all make your peace with everything that has been in your life, with your own conscience, with everyone around you, everyone that you have ever encountered, all the circumstances of your life, all your words and deeds, and with God. And so let's do it. Ask yourself about your immediate circle of relatives, friends, acquaintances, ask yourself – am I at peace with each of them? If you are not, find that peace.'

And he said: 'Yes, but there are people who are dead'. So I gave him the example which I gave you earlier about the man who had killed his beloved one. Thus we went through all his circle of people. There was a struggle! It was not an easy thing to do, but he found peace, and then moved on and on, uncovering one layer after another!

A Russian Divine said that clearing one's conscience is very similar to peeling an onion. To begin with, you rub the dry leaves; they go and there is no problem, but when you start to detach those which are still full of juice, you begin to weep and you cry and cry until you come to the very centre of the onion and you discover that the centre is sweet.

Well, that is what we did. We did that for three months in the course of which he went down and down. I remember that when he was really dying, a couple of weeks before he died, there was nothing left of him, except big shining eyes and the body which could not even hold a spoon to feed himself. He said to me, 'You know, my body is practically dead, and yet I have never been so intensely alive as I am now'.

Because he had discovered that this life did not depend on his physical condition, but on the wholeness which had become his, the abundance of life into which he had plunged, he could face death in a way in which he could not have faced it when he was still carrying the burden of the past, all the bitterness, the resentments, the pain, the revengeful feelings and all the alienation.

CHAPTER 4

Inner Resources for Growing Older

Helen Oppenheimer

Terms of Reference

Jane Austen's Mrs Elton in *Emma* is a brilliant caricature because her value judgements are not entirely false. They are merely so slanted by self-esteem as to be effectively preposterous. 'I have no fear of retirement,' she announced. 'Blessed with so many resources within myself, the world was not necessary to *me*. I could do very well without it. To those who had no resources it was a different thing; but my resources made me quite independent.'

As we grow older, we need to find out what the truth is like, of which Mrs Elton's pretentiousness is a travesty. If we live long enough we shall need to face retirement of a more drastic kind than the quiet life away from society which she envisages. What resources within ourselves do we have, to enable us to face the probably unwelcome prospect of leaving first youth, then middle age, behind?

The characteristic joys of ageing are maturity, confidence, long-standing friendships, having more time, perhaps having grandchildren. Truth forbids us to belittle the characteristic troubles of old age: loneliness, isolation, physical disability, loss of memory, saying goodbye.

Lord Hugh Cecil is said to have described old age as 'the out-patients' department of Purgatory'. There is a stage beyond maturity, the old old, which many people feel they would rather not reach. Being superseded by youngsters can be an affliction, but it is worse to see one's cherished ideas superseded, the history one has lived through rewritten and the values one has taken for granted abandoned.

Because of the acceleration of change in this century, old people cannot count on being thought wise. It is young people now who are expected to understand best what is going on. Once, if you were good and kind, you pitied little children and honoured the aged. Now you honour children and pity the aged: which is better than not honouring and not pitying, but probably less happy for everyone in the long run.

When we try to face the future we may find ourselves thinking: it is not old age as such which is alarming, but the slowness, the deafness, the forgetfulness, the ugliness, the helplessness, the loneliness. We associate all these miseries with old age, partly because if we live to be old our weaknesses have had plenty of time to show up.

What honesty without defeatism says is that these troubles, though sometimes characteristic of ageing, are neither confined to aged people nor inevitable. Any of them may afflict younger human beings too, and none of them is an essential feature of growing old. The longer we live, the more likely we are to experience some of them: but not all. *The Oxford Companion to the Mind* (Gregory 1987) is in fact quite reassuring: 'old age is a revealing time, when the best and the worst in us stand out in bold relief'. The joys, the miseries, the ordinariness of age are as variegated as the ups and downs of being young. The differences between old people remain far more important than their similarities.

Not many people are going to live a whole life without any 'thorn in the flesh' (2 Cor. 12:7). Moralists warn us not to rely on material resources: wealth cannot keep us young for ever. Some people are brave enough to invest in facelifts, maybe with encouraging results: but what can give us a life-lift? How can we find out how to live at peace with the terms of reference we have been given? On what resources can we draw?

More fundamental resources for human flourishing than material wealth are courage, companionship and faith. We can call them 'inner resources' if we like, not because they originate within ourselves, but because they become our own, unlike the kind of 'treasure on earth' (Matt. 6:19–21) which somebody might pick up and carry away.

Courage

We need courage because we need truth. In the long run it is no use to try to manage fear by fudging. Some terrors may vanish if we persuade ourselves that there is 'no cause for alarm'. Not all fears are groundless, though, and there are plenty of things which it is entirely reasonable to fear. Sooner or later it must be said that, if we are honest, there is no substitute for courage. To ask for truth is to face the fact that truth may turn out to be unpalatable, even to be what we most fear. But if we refuse to ask for truth we may be confronted by what we fear without having provided ourselves with any way of facing it.

C.S. Lewis said somewhere that courage is not a separate virtue but the form any virtue takes when seriously practised. Perhaps we shall never know whether we have the necessary courage until the time comes: but knowing that courage is what we need, looking steadily at real fears, not shying away from shadows, and getting all the encouragement we can from the company of other people, must all help.

We do not know what is in store for us. 'Honesty is the best policy' does not mean that we must face up to each possible unwelcome development as if it were about to happen. When we do not know what to expect we need another slogan, which is not, of course, contrary to honesty, but keeps an honest balance: 'Worrying is a bad policy.' Worry can be compared with mustard. It is said that mustard manufacturers make their money out of the mustard people leave on their plates. It could be said that the Devil gets rich from the worries people leave on their plates: the things they worry about which never happen. Dreadful things happen, but often what happens is not what people have been worrying about. Since worry is so often wasted, can we skip the worry and face real troubles rather than imaginary ones?

This does not mean neglecting to take precautions. On the contrary, we can take the precautions, just as we take out an insurance policy, instead of worrying. We do what we reasonably can and then live in the present where reality is to be met. C.S. Lewis was right here again. His senior devil in *The Screwtape Letters* pointed out to his young pupil that:

> real resignation, at the same moment, to a dozen different and hypothetical fates, is almost impossible, and the Enemy [God] does not greatly assist those who are trying to attain it: resignation to present and actual suffering, even when that suffering consists of fear, is far easier and is usually helped by His direct action. (Lewis 1942)

We may wonder whether we shall become deaf or blind or confused or cantankerous, but we are not expected to live with all that now, without access to the palliations or comforts which may come too. Tomorrow's distress cannot be faced, bravely or otherwise, until tomorrow has become today.

Worrying is a bad policy, not only because it makes us uncomfortable, but because it can lead straight into the thing we fear. Expectations are often self-fulfilling. 'I can't manage': I certainly cannot if I never try. 'I shall get feebler and feebler': maybe from lack of exercise. 'Nobody will love me': how can they, if I make myself so prickly? 'I'm helpless and hopeless': well, yes, if you say so. Surely there is nothing dishonest about keeping a look out for the gleam of light at the end of the dark tunnel.

It should be a good strategy to sort out our fears and deal with them piecemeal. Why is old age a problem? What are we afraid of? For some people, if they are honest, what they fear about old age is that it brings death nearer. We are sometimes told that there is no point in being afraid of death. We are given permission to fear old age, and directed to treat ageing as the real problem. It is true enough that we must find ways of facing old age. But there are people who fear old age mainly because it means the inevitable approach of death, and they must face *that* fear, not only some possibly easier substitute.

Death cannot be denied for ever. Its approach may be the more distressing in the end, now that it can be postponed and ignored for so long. There are ways of coming to terms with mortality by thinking of the rhythms of nature, autumn succeeding summer, and of the welcome contrasts of human life. As Spencer puts it in *The Faerie Queene,* 'Sleep after toil, port after stormy seas, ease after war, death after life does greatly please'. A secular funeral can be a moving experience, comforting to mourners when pious assurances, known to have meant little to the person who has died, cannot take hold.

To Christians, the Easter message is bound to be more encouraging, and the unbeliever's courage is hard to fathom. That is what one would expect, if it is true that courage can be found for the situation one is actually in, not for somebody else's situation which one might have been in. Truth about where one is and courage to cope with it are inextricably intertwined.

To sceptics, Christian courage may seem an easy matter of living by happy fables. Christians who believe that the stories are not fables may humbly recognise that they are fortunate: faith does make the human condition less alarming. They should not imagine that faith lets them off from needing courage at all. It is an aspect of Christian honesty to admit that faith may not abolish the fear of death. To set off alone on a journey to an unknown land, where we cannot take our human props but must take our human weaknesses and failures, demands courage.

Courage is not synonymous with stoicism. Jesus was not stoical in Gethsemane (Mark 14:32–37) and thereby set Christians a more en-couraging example. Followers of Christ are allowed to be afraid. They are allowed to admit that they mind about what happens and that what happens may fill them with dismay. The Christian hope is not that we shall escape the worst, nor that it will not hurt, but that if we can find the courage to go through the worst there is resurrection on the other side.

Company

For sceptics, there is no 'other side' beyond human life. Encouragement must come from one another. Human help is not as powerful as divine help, but for many people it appears easier to identify. Heaven forbid that Christians should belittle what human beings can do to help each other. At least we may be glad to realise that when our attention is focused upon ageing as part of life, not upon dying as leaving life behind, Christians and sceptics are not talking different languages. Human *companionship* can come into its own.

For companionship we look most naturally to people of our own age, but the older we get the fewer of these remain. It may not be quite true, in Charles Lamb's words, that, 'All, all are gone, the old familiar faces', but it is most likely to be true that older people need younger people more, both for sustenance and for encouragement.

Unless we can establish companionship between generations, many old people will be lonely. A great enemy of companionship is stereotyping, and the impoverishing divisions between age groups which come to seem natural. 'At her age, how could she understand how I feel?' and conversely, 'Young people today are so thoughtless'. The most insidious is not even stereotyping one another but stereotyping oneself. 'You can't teach an old dog new tricks.' 'This is how I've always done it.' Who can have authority to argue with the one whose life it is, who surely knows best? So people leave one another imprisoned in cages they have shut themselves into.

If we could do one single thing to make older people's lives happier, the best would be to stop the stereotyping and treat them as individuals. Old age can mean many different things. Old people differ at least as much as young people do. Some of them are timid and fragile, and some are defeatist; but many people as they grow older find themselves less fearful, less gauche, less worried by what other people think of them, than they were when they were young. Ageing is like making mayonnaise: one can put the oil into the egg more confidently, with less risk that the whole thing will curdle. The dear old lady may turn out to be less shockable than some of her juniors. Children growing up, who are used to their parents taking fright at their non-conformity, may expect their grandparents' generation to need even more shielding. They may be surprised to discover that old people, freed from the burden of total responsibility, can be unexpectedly receptive to new ideas.

Making friends between generations needs more effort than making friends with contemporaries. One starts with fewer shared assumptions. It may be like making friends with foreigners. There is a new language to be learnt, at least to comprehend, even though one would feel foolish to try to speak it. It is mildly embarrassing if Granny starts to say, 'That's cool'; and, by the time Granny has learnt to say it, that particular expression is probably out of date. What matters is not keeping up with trends, but refusing to settle down lazily in unexamined assumptions.

People who are fortunate enough to see their children's children have a particularly good chance, if they will take it, of being released from some of their stereotypes, and even of releasing the younger generation from some of theirs. Not only grandparents, but uncles and aunts, godparents and friends, who are privileged to share with parents the happy prejudice that these children are special, have a more relaxed opportunity than parents to stand back from the effort of making the next thing happen and positively enjoy the realisation of how special, how variegated and unexpected, children are even from their babyhood. Making friends with people much younger than oneself offers opportunities, not only to enjoy their company, but also to let them see that the old ones too are human beings, with distinctive characteristics, likes and dislikes, weaknesses and achievements.

One stereotype which hinders companionship is the one-sided cult of autonomy, which has become a tyranny. There is a new commandment: 'You must take control of your life'; and there are always plenty of people, old and young, who for many reasons cannot obey this command, and devalue themselves accordingly. One hears an ageing person say, 'I don't mind being old so long as I don't become dependent'. We know what that means; but rather than agreeing, it would be better to remember how dependent we all are.

Total autonomy is a fiction, and not an inspiring one. We all need each other all the time. The dependence of a hospital patient is different in degree but not in kind from the dependence of any of us upon the people who provide the services which keep us fed, warm, and in touch with each other. None of us could thrive without other people. If we set up autonomy as an obvious aim, we load an extra burden on vulnerable people, making them not only helpless but inadequate. W.H. Vanstone's fine book *The Stature of Waiting* (1982) is about the dignity of dependence and the need to redress the balance between our ideas of active and passive, especially in the light of the Passion of Christ.

Interdependence is a better keyword: dependence that goes both ways. Since we really do depend upon each other, acknowledging this fact is a strength not a weakness. Dependence is hardly ever a one-way street. Teachers say sincerely about pupils, 'They taught me as much as I taught them'. Most of us have had the experience of being comforted by people we were trying to comfort.

The most sadly dependent people are the ones who have lost their confidence: and what worse way to restore confidence than to reinforce people's helplessness by being relentlessly good to them? The poorest poor, said Wordsworth in his poem 'The old Cumberland beggar',

> Long for some moments in a weary life,
> When they can feel and know that they have been,
> Themselves, the fathers and the dealers-out
> Of some small blessings; have been kind to such
> As needed kindness, for this single cause
> That we have all of us one human heart.

A good way to make old people, or people of any age, happy is to keep alive their consciousness that they can make other people happy, and that being able to do this is part of our humanity.

Instead of saying, 'I'll see you get your rights', it can be more encouraging to say, 'Will you do me a favour?' We ought to be wary of the ultimately unconstructive attitude that 'human rights' are the supreme good. Rights are important as the answer to wrongs; but getting one's rights is a very small beginning towards flourishing as a human being, and may even be a distraction.

Faith

Christians are not called upon to belittle human companionship: on the contrary, they have found a way of humanising divine companionship. They find the grace of God brought down to earth in the form of an identifiable human being. Their justification for this move is that they trust the testimony of the people who were there that the life, death and resurrection of Jesus make a coherent story which supports the claim that God was in Christ. Part of what this means is that God is no absentee landlord but knows at first hand what it is like to live, and to die a horrible death, as a human being. For Christians the basis of encouragement is that what God expects of us, God has been willing to undergo.

Christians believe that God-made-man faced and overcame the horrors of betrayal, execution, pain, weakness, disappointment and abandonment. We cannot make room in the story for his sufferings to take precisely the form of what Teilhard de Chardin in *Le Milieu Divin* called the 'diminishments' of old age. Those of us who are past middle age are treading where the Lord did not tread. So what resources have we for this stage of our journey when we have to admit that the Lord has not been here?

We cannot make old age into a good thing simply by calling it good. We can choose whether to call the glass half empty or half full, but if it really is nearly empty it is no good deciding to call it full, and even worse to say, 'Water isn't real so we can call it what we like'. What we can say is that good and bad are generally mixed, and that we have some choice, indeed some responsibility, about which bits we pick out.

Neither good happenings nor bad happenings are final. Everything needs to be made good. The only thing that is wrong with 'They lived happily ever after' is that it makes a beginning sound like an end. If we impose an unrealistic finality upon young people's new beginnings, it is even more tempting to make that mistake with the later part of people's lives. Re-tirement, slowing down, leaving one's home and moving somewhere more manageable, are just as much beginnings as leaving school or starting a new job. Of course we ask, 'Is this the right thing to do?' The answer is, 'To be certain, you need to live it out. You can say that it looks promising. Whether it will turn out to have been right depends on what you make of it.'

In 'making good', faith has a large part to play. What faith does is seize on the best and give it a chance. Human faith can do a lot. To believe that good can come even out of the very worst needs more than human faith. When we look at some of the troubles human beings have and how some people end their days, and ask what good can come, then all we can say is 'God knows' how this can be put right. If one is fortunate enough to have Christian faith one need not say 'God knows' bitterly. In the light of the Cross and the Resurrection a Christian can honestly say, first, 'God does know: God has joined in', and then 'All things are possible with God'.

The most fundamental Christian belief is that adversity can be not only bearable but redeemable. The principle of death and resurrection is at the heart of Christianity. Nor is this foreign to ordinary human life. What we grab we spoil; what we let go may come back to us in a better form. Whatever old age is like, it is likely to be practice in letting go; and people who learn how to let go generously, not grudgingly, are taking the first steps towards resurrection.

There is a lofty word 'contemplation' which very active people know is above them. To be forced to let go could be an unaccustomed kind of grace, almost as if the Lord were teasing one gently and saying, 'Stop thinking you can't learn this'. Retired people take courses in all sorts of things they thought they would never do. Perhaps the compulsory slowing up of ageing is a sort of elementary course in the art of living in the present. Can people who have always been inclined to rush about and not stop to appreciate, who have always been short of time, who know perfectly well that we ought to attend more to things and to one another, learn how to make something positive out of the necessity to take on less and go more slowly?

When people have to retire because they are too old to work, must they be stuck in idleness, which has no point and is bound to pall? The opposite of work need not be uselessness, or even rest: it might be *play*. If people are working, they can be asked, 'What is the point of it?' and the answer will be something like, 'To make a living', 'To satisfy my boss', 'To benefit humanity', 'To fulfil my vocation'. Work has to have a point or it is soul-destroying, but play is its own point.

To enter the Kingdom of Heaven we are supposed to 'become as little children' (Mark 10:15) and we imagine unrealistically that this must mean 'be innocent'. The conspicuous thing about children is not their innocence, but their play. They concentrate wholeheartedly and unselfconsciously on doing things for fun, without assuming that what we do always needs some justification beyond itself. Could we stop using 'second childhood' as a euphemism for senility? If being 'young in heart' when we are old means something good, not just a refusal to admit the passage of time, it means being able to enter into the happy spirit of play. It means keeping, or regaining, a heavenly and self-forgetful light-heartedness, which maturity does not require us to outgrow. There is an image in the Book of Genesis (Gen. 3:8) which has been lost in all the emphasis on apples and disobedience: 'They heard the voice of the Lord God walking in the garden in the cool of the day'. Human beings were meant to join in this evening walk, to enjoy the company of their Maker.

CHAPTER 5

One Quaker's Perspective

Muriel Bishop Summers

Is there a Quaker view of the spirituality of ageing? As I read through the Advices and Queries, designed to help us examine our spiritual life and to challenge us in its outworking, those pertinent sentences which form part of the book *Quaker Faith and Practice* (1994), I am struck by several which are applicable to every stage of our life journey, including ageing. The following are a selection:

> Bring the whole of your life under the ordering of the spirit of Christ. Are you open to the healing power of God's love? Cherish that of God within you, so that this love may grow in you and guide you. Let your worship and your daily life enrich each other. Treasure your experience of God, however it comes to you ... (1.02 2)

> Every stage of our lives offers fresh opportunities. Responding to divine guidance, try to discern the right time to undertake or relinquish responsibilities without due pride or guilt. Attend to what love requires of you, which may not be great busyness. (1.02 28)

> Approach old age with courage and hope. As far as possible make arrangements for your care in good time, so that an undue burden does not fall on others. Although old age may bring increasing disability and loneliness, it can also bring serenity, detachment and wisdom. Pray that in your final years you may be enabled to find new ways of receiving and reflecting God's love. (1.02 29)

Only one of these statements refers specifically to ageing, although each, and others in Quaker Advices and Queries, could do so. I know that I would be well advised to study and reflect on them regularly.

It sounds so easy! But, in my own experience and through talking with other elders, I know that the process of getting old is not, necessarily, easy. When I was a child I thought my parents and their friends were old. As I grew up I hardly considered 'getting old' as a possibility or a reality for myself; it was something happening to other people. Even now, at the age of 76, forced to recognise some loss of physical ability, some unwanted physical discomfort (yes, pain!) and increasing slowness of mind, I am often reluctant to admit to ageing. Why is that? Have I learned that being old is unacceptable in our society?

During the past few years, I have been privileged to co-lead workshops for older women. One of our early tasks was to name the stereotyping of older people: redundant, past 'sell-by' date, useless, to be pitied, limited – and other titles more cruel and dismissive. Following this we examined how we ourselves often 'bought into' those stereotypes, however much we really didn't believe them. We even laughed about them and about ourselves as we set about reclaiming our power and the dignity which such stereotyping can strip from us. In the process we learned much. It was, in truth, a spiritual exercise, recognising how deeply negative images restrict us and limit our potential – whatever our age or circumstance.

'Ageing itself isn't the problem,' point out Rabbi Zalman Schachter-Shalomi and Ronald Miller in their book *From Age-ing to Sage-ing* (1995), 'It's the images we hold about it, our cultural expectations, that cause our problems'. This is in no way to diminish or deny the reality of physical hardship or mental diminishment, rather to encourage us to 'change our ageing paradigm, the model or blueprint that determines the quality of our experience'.

What does 'spirituality in ageing' require of me? What does it offer me?

I recognise how little I know about the negative aspects of ageing. I am blessed with relatively good health, able to be more active than many people of the same age. Although I have experienced loss of dear relatives and friends, remarriage at the age of 70 means that for the time being I am blessed with intimate companionship. I unite with the author of *Moving On*, Kathleen Fischer, when she writes:

> I have learned how difficult it is to talk about an experience as diverse as aging. Is it the best of times or the worst of times? An effort to stress the positive side of aging can mask its adversities. A focus on the problems of aging can obscure its possibilities. (Fischer 1996, p.2)

I could do worse than continue to quote Fischer or Schachter-Shalomi but commend both authors to your own reading! Instead let me share some of my own discoveries.

Quakers do not separate the sacred from the secular: 'Bring the *whole* [emphasis added] of your life under the ordering of the spirit of Christ'.

It is, therefore, as important to care for the body, God's temple, as for the spirit; right to keep as fit and healthy as possible, ensuring activities and enjoyable diet as is appropriate for one's physical condition.

(I admit that I find it hard to keep to my diabetic diet and must remind myself that doing so is both a physical and a spiritual discipline.) As I become less physically able I try to find alternative activities, more gentle exercise, and breathing techniques. These, I believe, aid the body and encourage a quieter, more reflective mind.

As I grow older I notice a stronger desire to practise stillness. My time of quiet in the mornings becomes more precious with a deeper longing to carry the Presence with me throughout the day. A desire to 'rest in the Lord', to wait patiently... to be willing to surrender, to let go. How hard that is, both to determine what it is that must be released, whether of outward activities or inward yearnings, and then to actually 'let go'. Do I even need to 'let go of letting go'? Is that an essential part of resting in God's arms? At the same time I recognise a horrid increase in my irritability and intolerance. Is this part of the ageing process or a spiritual battle to be won? I therefore find myself identifying with that anonymous Seventeenth-century Nun's Prayer:

> LORD Thou knowest better than I know myself that I am growing older and will some day be old. Keep me from the fatal habit of thinking I must say something on every subject and on every   occasion. Release me from craving to straighten out everybody's   affairs. Make me thoughtful but not moody: helpful but not bossy.   With my vast store of wisdom, it seems a pity not to use it all, but   Thou knowest Lord that I want a few friends at the end.
>
> Keep my mind free from the recital of endless details; give me wings to get to the point. Seal my lips on my aches and pains. They are increasing, and love of rehearsing them is becoming sweeter as the years go by. I dare not ask for grace enough to enjoy the tales of others' pains, but help me to endure them with patience.
>
> I dare not ask for improved memory, but for a growing humility and a lessing cocksureness when my memory seems to clash with the memories of others. Teach me the glorious lesson that occasionally I may be mistaken.

Keep me reasonably sweet; I do not want to be a Saint – some of them are so hard to live with – but a sour old person is one of the crowning works of the devil. Give me the ability to see good things in unexpected places, and talents in unexpected people. And, give me, O Lord, the grace to tell them so.

AMEN

Much as I love the practice of Quaker worship framed in silence, I realise that music and the ritual of spoken liturgy enrich my life. Theology itself becomes less important to me – the boundaries of my faith expand as I recognise more fully the various ways in which God is revealed or speaks in the hearts of humankind. Rabbi Schachter-Shalomi points out in *Age-ing and Sage-ing*: 'According to the Kabbalah, God wears a multitude of masks, clothing itself in divine images that we can apprehend with our finite minds'. (Schachter-Shalomi and Miller 1995, p.146)

This is a time of my life when I can look back, celebrating much of the past, accepting with regret any errors or wasted opportunities – and then letting them go. Time also to consider what needs attention in my personal affairs, such as updating my will, considering plans for the unknown future, clearing, while I am able, the clutter of belongings and, importantly, forgiving and accepting forgiveness as it is needed. All part of the spiritual journey.

I spoke earlier of the workshops given for older women (we titled them 'The Time of Your Life'). During these we found that rich exploration involved 'looking back' and 'looking forward'. The first of these considered 'harvesting'. Naming the wisdom we had learned and what fruits we could garner from our often hard-won experience of living. What core of our experience would we want to share with those following us? Could we create a wisdom legacy? We also wondered how to convey that rich legacy in a manner which would not confine or shackle those to whom we might leave it but rather free and enable them.

You may remember something I knew, years ago, as a 'guzzunder', a useful article originally designed as a night-pot, kept under the bed for use during those long hours to save trotting to the outhouse. Such guzzunders were often ceramic and beautifully decorated. Nowadays they seldom serve their original purpose – instead they often have bulbs planted in them, giving rise to beauty and delight, in a creative use of an older purpose. Can we allow our 'truths' and traditions to be valued yet to change and evolve into different and perhaps more beautiful and contemporary experiences of God's truth?

The second exploration was framed by the question, 'When the Visitor [Death] knocks at the door, what gift will you give him?' Most of us agreed that to offer 'a completed life' was our desire and we pondered how to achieve it. Can we face the prospect of death with open-hearted acceptance? Can we also face the years of ageing joyfully and with hope, in spite of its immediate or potential problems?

The hope offered me during these years is encapsulated in the verses from Psalm 139 and Psalm 23:5 (NEB):

> Whither shall I go from thy spirit? or whither shall I flee from thy presence? If I ascend up into heaven thou are there; if I make my bed in hell thou art there. If I take the wings of the morning, and dwell in the uttermost parts of the sea: Even there shall thy hand lead me, and thy right hand hold me.

> 'Thou spreadest a table before me in the sight of my enemies. Thou has richly bathed my head oil, and my cup runs over.'

> In my ageing process I come to realise the varied forms 'my enemies' might take: disablement, loneliness, fear amongst them. Then I try to visualise the table God has prepared for me, wondering what is spread there for my sustenance – the harvest of the Spirit perhaps? Love, joy, peace, patience... (Gal. 5:22)

For each person the process of ageing may be different, our expression of its spirituality varied, and perhaps changing, yet may the certainty of the Presence be increasingly real for us all.

CHAPTER 6

The Lord's Prayer
A Prayer of the Ageing
James A. Crampsey SJ

The Lord's Prayer is a prayer that anyone can make. In the Gospels, Jesus invites us to make this prayer our own and it is the best-known and most frequently used prayer in Christianity. It is therefore not a prayer which is exclusive to the ageing, but I have chosen it as a prayer which the ageing person can make for a number of reasons. First of all, because it is familiar to everyone; second, because one of the things I hear from the elderly is that they find it difficult to pray because they find it difficult to concentrate for very long. This is all the more distressing if the person is unable to get to church. Third, I think it addresses some key issues for elderly people, especially in the second half of the prayer: issues such as anxiety, forgiveness and judgement. The aim of this chapter then is to take the Lord's Prayer and to focus on it as a prayer which the ageing can especially make their own.

The Setting of the Prayer in Matthew

The Lord's Prayer in Matthew is part of the Sermon on the Mount (Matt. 5–7), and before Jesus teaches us to pray, He makes two criticisms of other ways of praying:

> And when you pray, you must not be like the hypocrites; for they love to stand and pray in the synagogue and at street corners, that they may be seen. Truly I say to you, they have their reward. But when you pray, go into your room and shut the door and pray to your Father who is in secret, and your Father who sees in secret will reward you. (6:5–6)

I am less concerned here with the negative criticism than with the positive recommendation of that quiet and personal relationship with the Father which is there for us wherever we are. We do not need to go to public worship to find God in prayer. The second criticism goes as follows:

> And in praying do not heap up empty phrases as the Gentiles do: for they think that they will be heard for their many words. Do not be like them, for your Father knows what you need before you ask him.

Perhaps here there is a note of comfort for those who feel that they cannot pray for as long a time as they used to.[1] Prayer is the name we give to those moments in our lives when we allow our desire to be with God to hold the centre stage. Prayer is what we call the meeting between God's desire for us and our desire for God. 'Your Father knows what you need before you ask him.' And what we all need in our lives is a sense of God's love for us. This mutual desire is strongly present in the prayer itself. If love at its deepest frees the other person to be who he or she is, then the first half of the prayer expresses our love and desire that God be God in the fullest sense. The second half of the prayer asks God to free us from those elements in our life which prevent us from being what God wants us to be, that is most fully ourselves as God's creation.

Ourselves as God's Creation

Before starting on the Lord's Prayer proper, it might help if some consideration was given to the theme of ourselves as God's creation. What does the Bible say about the human being who ages? Is ageing to be welcomed or feared? The Hebrew Scriptures have a variety of perspectives on the subject (on this material, see Wolff 1974, pp.119–127). On the one hand, the accounts of the deaths of the heroes show that old age is a sign of living life to its full and content completion. 'Abraham breathed his last and died in a good old age, an old man and full of years and was gathered to his people' (Gen. 25:7–8).

Again on the positive side, old age is a time when a person expects to be a repository of wisdom; reflection on experience makes him or her a good teacher of those younger. 'Wisdom is with the aged and understanding in length of days' (Job 12:12).

On the other hand ageing is also experienced as a time of diminishment, most brilliantly expressed in Ecclesiastes 12:1–12. The pessimism of this

---

1   I am not saying that it is useless to spend time in prayer. I would be going against the weight of the learned experience of the Christian tradition on prayer, which I respect.

allegory[2] must not be mistaken for realism. For a central belief about God in the Hebrew Scriptures is that God can overturn the expectations of what life is to be like in old age. The most striking example is the birth of Isaac when both Abraham and Sarah are incapable of having a child. Moses is also said to have transcended the limitations of age: 'Moses was a hundred and twenty years old when he died; his eye was not dim nor his natural force abated' (Deut. 34:7). But it is not just the great heroes for whom this happens. Psalm 92 praises the righteous who flourish like a palm tree, and in v. 14 says:

> They still bring forth fruit in old age They are ever full of sap and green to show that Yahweh is upright.

And again Isaiah shows how trust in Yahweh can bring about a reversal in the expected state of affairs:

> Even youths shall faint and be weary and young warriors shall fall exhausted. But they who hope in Yahweh shall renew their strength. They mount up with wings like eagles. (Isaiah 40:30)

Theologically, what we can say is that old age is part of God's plan for human beings; this is seen from the texts about the heroes who have lived life to its completion, and the recognition that in old age, people have an important role as the bearers of their community's lived experience formulated as wisdom. There are also two late prophetic texts which envisage the new reality which God will bring about as distinguished by living to a good old age. This is God's plan, this is what he desires for us:

> No more shall be heard in it [Jerusalem] the sound of weeping and the cry of distress. No more shall there be in it an infant that lives but a few days, or an old man who does not fill out his days. For the child shall die a hundred years old, and the sinner a hundred years old shall be accursed. (Isaiah 65:19–20)[3]

Zechariah 8:4 presents a more contemplative picture: 'Thus says the Lord of Hosts: Old men and old women shall again sit in the streets of Jerusalem, each with staff in hand for very age.'

---

2   For a full explanation see Wolff (1974), p.123f. Starting with 12:3, the parts of the body which experience diminishment are discussed in this order: arms, legs, teeth, eyes, ears gone deaf, the voice, hair turns grey, walking is difficult, aphrodisiacs useless.

3   This assumes that sinners die young, and that even a sinner ought to live for more than a hundred years.

But together with this optimistic picture runs an acknowledgement of the reality that old age involves diminishment of one's physical and psychological powers. Thus there is a reality acknowledged and a hope expressed, and both of these are undergirded by a conviction that God can reverse the expectation of old age as continual decline. Old age can also be a time of renewal, where God can bring about something unexpected in the life of a person. Perhaps we can rule out what happens to Abraham and Sarah, but we can very well see the possibility of new insight, new syntheses and new ways of experiencing the reality of God in our lives. If we do not hold this, then we are already settling for society's evaluation of the ageing as people for whom nothing significant happens any more.

Work and Rest

Part of such an evaluation has to do with a mistaken priority which is ascribed to the producers in society to the detriment of those who are non-producers. The fact that the non-producers feel guilty about not working or producing is simply a testimony to the pervasive character of this sense of values. This view needs to be challenged, and a radical challenge can be found in the biblical teaching about the Sabbath: the relationship between work and rest.[4]

There are two central texts about the reason for Sabbath in Torah. The first is from Exodus 20:8–11 and in this passage the Sabbath is a consequence of God's own creative activity. God has arranged time in such a way as to build rest into the very structure of His created order and so as to oblige humanity to rest. This is not an optional extra, but it is the way things are meant to be.

The second text is from Deuteronomy 5:12–15. Here the emphasis is social, that is the way God's plan is expressed in the just dealings among people. Human beings need rest, and especially servants need rest. This is written in the heart of Israel's sense of justice, because God liberated them from the oppressive servitude in Egypt. The Sabbath here is a prophetic statement against any understanding that people are to be identified with work, and it is the condition of servitude where this is most likely to happen. Human beings are not instruments, and work is not the be-all and end-all of a person.

---

4   In what follows, I am indebted to the treatment of Walter Harrelson, *The Ten Commandments and Human Rights* (1980), pp.79–105.

Theologically, God is the one in whom a person finds his or her identity, and to establish one's identity in anything short of God is simply idolatry. Thus this third commandment of the decalogue about the Sabbath's holiness is of a piece with the first two which demand an exclusive loyalty to God. If work is necessary to sustain the life of the community, the Sabbath is even more necessary to acknowledge that it is God in the end who sustains the life of the community. The Sabbath is God's gift to the people to allow them to take their rest and find their strength in their God. But the single most important element in our discussion here is that it emerges that it is rest which gives the true perspective on work. And for us, it is important to be able to define work in relation to rest, not the other way round. Work is a cessation of rest. Our relaxing in God has to be broken off in order for us to perform our necessary tasks, but these while important are secondary. It is interesting that when we consider the portrayal of life in the Garden of Eden, the sin of Adam and Eve is discovered when God is taking a relaxing stroll in the cool of the evening and wants them to accompany him and enjoy it with him. God has to ask 'Where are you?' The sin, of course, brings about a disharmony between God and the couple, but also a disharmony between them and the created order. Genesis certainly presents work as something which is not always going to give pleasure to the worker, even if it does not go so far as to call work sinful. I wonder whether it would be correct to understand the guilt feelings we have when we are not working, or the listlessness we feel when we are inactive, as part of the legacy of this disharmony with creation which has somehow programmed into us a skewed understanding of the relationship between rest and work.

Finally, the fourth commandment has a contribution to make on this theme too. We may have been too successful in our catechism by presenting 'Honour thy father and thy mother' as a commandment which is the concern of young children and adolescents. In reality, it has much more to do with the way adults relate to aged and unproductive parents. How we treat the elderly is a barometer of family life and, by extension, of whether there is justice in our society. These relationships are our mutual responsibility because our relationships are sustained by the one whom Jesus invites us to call Father.

Father

The whole of the Lord's Prayer is only possible because of the way it begins. In the words of the liturgy, we dare to call God 'Father'. The God Jesus reveals to us, for all His majesty, can be spoken about and spoken to by means of a familiar word with its associations of personal and significant relationship. In the twentieth century we have perhaps recovered a sense of God which makes this language about Him meaningful. At the same time, the language itself is not without its contemporary difficulties. People who have had bad experiences of human parenting cannot use this language very easily; there has also been sufficient research which has recovered traditional ways of imaging God as Mother and this has been an enrichment of our language about God. There are always difficulties in talking precisely about God, since God is the one who both must be spoken about, and cannot be spoken about, and our words are not adequate to describe who God is. Jesus invites us to understand our relationship with God as that of child to parent, so what resonances, what associations does Jesus' way of speaking about God have for those who are ageing?

One area that could be explored in this connection is that of bereavement. Ageing is a time when a person finds him or herself increasingly alone. One's contemporaries and perhaps one's spouse have died, or are ailing and cannot communicate. Sometimes, one's children and grandchildren no longer come to visit. All the people who have given me a sense of who I am, my identity, are no longer there. This can be distressing, disorienting and even frightening for a person. Calling on God in the way in which Jesus invites us to asks us to take seriously the fact that who we are, our identity, is given by God and cannot be taken away from us. Second, it recalls that our relationships with all God's daughters and sons are ultimately held together by God. Whatever is valuable in them will be sustained even though the human links seem tenuous or broken.

Again, rather like the relationship between rest and work, it is a matter of perspective. It is because God loves us that we are able to love one another. But sometimes we are so busy with our human relationships that we cannot see the truth of that. It is also worth thinking about Jesus in this context. The story of the Passion, particularly in Mark's gospel, tells of how Jesus becomes completely isolated from all the people He knows. Of those He has chosen, one friend betrays Him, one denies that he knows Him, the others run away: He is alone, exposed to the hostility and violence of the people who now gather round in a parody of intimacy. It is in that experience that He understands most deeply who the Father is, and that He is the Son. It does not seem too much to say that the political expediency, the self-interest and the matter-of-fact brutal violence which crucified Jesus have been repeated throughout history, and are present in our 'civilised' society in the way our ageing population suffers. The suffering of these men and women is written in God's heart, because Jesus has suffered in the same way. The challenge to our society is whether we can look at the crucifixion of God's sons and daughters, and be changed by it to the extent that we will not tolerate it. If we are looking for a starting point for a home-grown liberation theology, then we may not have too far to look.

Hallowed be thy name, thy kingdom come, thy will be done on earth as it is in heaven

Liberation is involving ourselves in an activity which ultimately only God can bring about, and all of these wishes express a desire that God do something which only God can do. As I said earlier, each of these wishes expresses our loving desire that God be God in the fullest sense, and that involves God being recognised as God by His creation, recognised as holy and praised for it. When we pray 'Hallowed be thy name', we are asking God to help us to be holy too, since as God's children we are to share in God's holiness. God's holiness is a reminder that God is the measure of what human beings have made of his creation, and is a challenge to us not to find our identity in the world's values, but in God.

For those who are ageing, would it be true to say that they have seen the world's values change? Can they be in a privileged position to see that the world's values are not absolute, and can they be freer of the short-sightedness of those of us who are immersed in our contemporary culture? Approaching the end of life's journey, are the ageing able to see the goal more clearly, and rejoice and praise the name of God who stands over against the world's values, and gladly desire to share in the making holy of God's name by the way they live their own lives?

When we pray 'Thy Kingdom come', we are praying that God act definitively to establish a state of affairs where the creation recognises God's kingly rule over human life and existence. If we as Christians make this prayer our own, then we are committing ourselves to the values of God's kingdom. We might sum these up by reference to the Beatitudes where the poor, meek, sorrowful and persecuted are pronounced blessed. This does not mean they are all right really. It means that they are the ones to whom God directs His love with a special tenderness. God does this because they are most in need; when Jesus pronounces them 'blessed', it is a challenge to us to see that need, be moved by it and act upon it. Very often those who are ageing can find themselves in the conditions described by the Beatitudes. What is fundamental here is that they are invited to enter into the understanding that they are especially and tenderly loved by God. This is all the more important, since people often have a tendency to blame themselves when they find themselves in the conditions called 'blessed'. How often do we hear ourselves and others saying, 'I must have done something wrong to be punished by God in this way'. For an ageing person, this can be frightening and seen as a sample of the punishment they can expect after death.

Thy will be done on earth as it is in heaven

Again this is a wish that God's plan be brought to fulfilment. When I listen to this phrase of the Lord's Prayer, I hear an echo of the Old Testament phrase, 'God's ways are not our ways'. This echo is reinforced when we hear the prayer of Jesus in the Agony in the Garden, Matthew 26:42, 'not my will but your will be done'. I think that this phrase of the Lord's Prayer especially acknowledges the mystery of God, and challenges us to accept that we may not know exactly where we fit into God's plan. Like Jesus himself, we may find ourselves in difficult situations to which we can only respond with trust and faithfulness. As Jesus says to Peter at the end of the Fourth Gospel, 'when you are old, someone else will gird you and carry you where you do not wish to go'. I think that we do the ageing a disservice when we pat them on the arm and say, 'Everything will be all right'. In a way we do that to make ourselves feel better. The ageing have a right to our being honest enough to acknowledge that we don't know: this honesty also acknowledges the mystery of the God we are praying to here.

When we move into the second half of the prayer, there is a change of focus indicated by the use of the word 'us'. As I mentioned above, these three petitions revolve around three themes which especially concern the ageing: anxiety, forgiveness and judgement.

Anxiety: Give us this day our daily bread

'Daily' here means the bread which we need to live. For the Christian, as he or she prays this phrase, it suggests the Eucharist as well as the bread which we need for our bodily needs. But fundamentally this prayer is one of trust in God that we will receive the necessities of life from the one who cares for us. It is often thought that another passage in the sixth chapter of Matthew is a commentary on this part of the Lord's Prayer. In Matthew 6:25–34, Jesus talks of the birds of the air and the lilies of the field to illustrate the point that life is more than food, and the body more than clothing. The message is one which tells us not to be anxious about such things because God knows that we need them all. This is both beautiful poetry and extremely difficult teaching. It seems to challenge the need that human beings have to plan, and invites us to take a rather reckless approach to everyday living. But as John Meier (1980) points out in his commentary on Matthew, Jesus does not forbid concern about physical needs, but rather the anxiety which expresses an unhealthy preoccupation about this world's goods. The disciple's life in the present must not be shaped by the fleeting future of tomorrow, but by the absolute future of the coming kingdom. Jesus makes the same point in the parable of the rich fool in Luke 12:15–21, where the landowner plans his future without any concern as to what God's future plan is for him. Now when we look at this part of the prayer, and what Jesus says on the same theme, what relevance has it for the ageing person?

An ageing person can be in a privileged position; it may well be that they find themselves in a situation where they do not need to plan for the future. The effect of this can be rather like the Sabbath properly understood. They have the opportunity to reflect on God's presence to them and their presence to God as they experience it today, here and now. They are perhaps free of the distraction of the future and its possibilities, in a way in which younger people are not. Younger people can escape from the present by saying for example, 'Once I've made my first million, that'll be me'; 'Once I get my own parish, that'll be me' or 'Once I get my children through school, that'll be me'. It is an interesting phrase, 'that'll be me': it is really what the rich fool says in the parable just referred to. It is saying that my identity is tied up with my future in such a way that it distracts me from who I am here and now. And really it is who I am here and now which will lay down the lines of who I will be, and once again it is important to have these elements in the correct order of priority. Those who are ageing, if they are freed from the distraction of the future, can concentrate on finding themselves and coming to terms with the God who loves them for who they are now.

But many ageing people are in fact paralysed by anxiety. 'Will my pensions and savings be enough to meet my needs?' 'If I get really ill, who will care for me?' 'Will I have to leave my home with all its memories and be put somewhere else?' 'Am I a burden to other people?' When Jesus invites us to make this part of the prayer our own, He is not saying that some kind of magical solution will occur. He is asking us to hold our very real concerns within a relationship with our God which is distinguished by trust: a trust that whatever our difficulties are, God is faithful to His covenant with us. As Isaiah says, 'Do not be afraid, for I have redeemed you, I have called you by your name, you are mine' (43:1–2). Still, Jesus is warning us that our legitimate concern must not become an anxiety where the future frightens us so much that it overwhelms us, and takes away our freedom to recognise and respond to God's presence in our lives. Anxiety can easily become despair which means that God cannot make Himself heard above the turmoil of our self-preoccupation.

Forgiveness: Forgive us our trespasses as we forgive those who trespass against us

The most striking feature of this element of the Lord's Prayer is that it is the only place where we seemingly have a two-way street. Of course, each of the elements of the Lord's Prayer presupposes some response or involvement on our part, but here our response is precisely and explicitly prescribed. Now we can hear this element of the prayer in a way which makes it sound like a deal between ourselves and God. 'I'll forgive John and Mary, if you'll forgive me, then we are quits!' I think such an understanding puts a false emphasis on the petition. The parable of the unforgiving servant in Matthew 18:21–35 is a more accurate guide to the meaning.

This familiar parable tells of the King remitting the fabulous and unpayable debt of the first servant in response to the desperate cry, 'Have patience with me, and I will pay you'. But when the second servant uses the same words to the first servant to whom he owes a trifling amount, the one who was let off does not even hear the echo of his own desperate plea and his narrow escape, and has the man thrown into prison. What is central here is that the experience of being forgiven has not taken root in such a way that he can forgive another. So, when we pray this element of the Lord's Prayer, we are saying that the forgiveness we have experienced and hope to experience from God is embodied in us as we deal with one another.

For the ageing person, forgiveness can be a central issue as a person mulls over his or her past life, and considers memories that are painful or relationships which are broken. There can be either a sense of unfinished business or of an unhealed wound. People often experience in prayer a surge of a painful or unpleasant memory which can be an apparent distraction from our attempt to be alone with God. But often these memories arise because we are unhappy with them and are asking God to heal them, and asking God to help us co-operate in that healing. The past can unsettle the present as much as the future can, and it may be that some aspects of the past are more alive for those who are ageing. But it may also be true that a person looking at incidents in his or her own life cannot believe that God will forgive them. At that point it may be worth looking at incidents where I was able to forgive someone, or someone else was able to forgive me although I had badly wronged them. How much more will God be able to forgive us if we desire His forgiveness. The experience of forgiving or being forgiven is in some way an entry into God's life. An inability to forgive myself is a form of idolatry where I make myself greater than God.

Judgement: And lead us not into temptation, but deliver us from evil

This petition expresses the same prayer both negatively and positively. 'Temptation' here is understood to be the final testing, rather than everyday temptation, and 'evil' probably should be understood as the evil one rather than general evil. This is a prayer with which we faithfully persevere in order to reach our true home in God, where God desires us to be. This then is a prayer that our desire to be with God be fulfilled and not thwarted.

Nevertheless, this prayer is often qualified or made half-heartedly, because for many people and in my experience for ageing people, meeting God is seen first and foremost in terms of judgement.

This theme occurs in many of the parables, but I want to take a brief look at one here to illuminate this question, and that is the parable of the sheep and the goats in Matthew 25:31–46. There is a clear separation of people here made vivid in our imagination in many works of art, notably that of Michaelangelo in the Sistine Chapel. The criterion of the separation is whether a person did or did not attend to the fundamental needs of God's people. Jesus is in such solidarity with God's people that, in them, He has or has not been ministered to.

From the point of view of the person who is ageing, this can present some difficulties. If they hear this text anew and, in looking back over their lives, can find no time when they ministered to those in need, are they supposed to remedy that now? What if they are housebound or incapacitated in other ways? Can they put this demand into practice? Perhaps one way of approaching the difficulty would be to encourage the ageing to pray in solidarity for those in need. But more importantly it seems to me that the ageing often are the hungry, thirsty, naked, sick and imprisoned, and what the parable is asking them to do is to recognise that Jesus is in utter solidarity with them as they experience these things. And in that recognition, there is no fear of judgement, because judgement is a separation from Christ and He is saying that He belongs to these people and that they belong to Him.

Conclusion

The biblical perspective on ageing envisages old age as a time of completion and fulfilment accompanied by the experience of diminishment. This tension is to be held in balance by a correct understanding of the relationship between rest and work, with rest to be seen as a privileged opportunity of relaxing with the God who desires our companionship. The obligation on family and society is to create the conditions where that kind of relaxation with God is possible. Jesus' teaching on prayer is an invitation to us to celebrate God's desire for us and our desire for God. Thus He invites us to identify with God's desire to be God for the creation, and to face up to those things in our lives which can inhibit our desire for God. Above all, God's desire for us has been made concrete in the person of Jesus Christ who has entered the depths of our pain and fear and loneliness, and continues in solidarity with those who are suffering. Finally, the Bible teaches us that for those who are old, God can still bring about something new and transforming in their lives, as with Abraham and Sarah, Zachary and Elizabeth, Simeon and Anna. They were able to tell of what the Lord had done for them, and so make possible the faith of those who come after them. This is the gift which we can receive from the ageing if only we have ears to hear.

everybody expecting me to just wind down and disintegrate' to
ful, conscious ripening, with a revitalising sense of focus and
place from which to harvest the fruits of a lifetime.

der people, according to Rabbi Schachter-Shalomi, feel a kind of
ay be disguised as boredom, but underneath it is a nagging sense
s more I have to know, there is something I have to become. I am
to submit the rest of my life to diminishing physical capacity.'
re, there is the worry: 'How will I spend my last years, without
ig a drag on me or my loved ones?' Many older people have been
from the French *retirer* – literally pulled away, from the work that
mething to them. They are more often asked what they have retired
an what they have retired for.

there are aches and pains. Often these are the pains of unlived life,
ring voices in the body saying, 'You haven't done this or that. You
roken promises to yourself.' Parts of us scream, because they have been
ed, when we didn't follow our bliss/our purpose/our destiny. Taking
illers to silence such regrets and longings, says Rabbi Schachter-
mi, is just like ripping out the cord of a ringing telephone. The message
ital one, and it will try any which way to get through until we listen to it.

We can, says Rabbi Schachter-Shalomi, meet approaching age and
reasing physical strength with denial. Alternatively, we can 'reach for the
ources that have begun to ripen, quietly, in another part of the inner
rden'. We can take hold of the energy of our anxieties, and utilise it for a
w unfolding, to begin what can be the most creative phase of our lives –
nd has indeed been recognised to be so, in other cultures and other times.
The problem, of course, is that most of us lack good role models for
becoming what Rabbi Schachter-Shalomi calls an 'Elder'. No one has taught
us how to handle this phase of life; no one has prepared us. We need initiation
into the work of Eldering.

Part of this work, says Rabbi Schachter-Shalomi, is repairing the wounds
of the past. And part of it is sifting and synthesising the lessons and events of
our lives, both those perceived as failures and those seen as successes, into
that distillation we call wisdom. Rabbi Schachter-Shalomi calls this work
'The Ministry of Spiritual Eldering', for this is *the* season of life for doing the
spiritual work of contemplation, meditation, forgiveness and letting go. It is
about making what Rabbi Schachter-Shalomi calls the 'mind-moves from
Ageing to Sageing' – becoming a sage, or wise one.

C

Harvestin

Jenny G

A New Paradigm of Ageing

There is something that all of us are doing
do we live this process? Will we experience o
problem or as opportunity?

We are perhaps the first generation to confi
massive scale. Our extended lifespan and th
combined to form an 'agewave', an unprecedente
now entering their autumn years. It becomes cru
perhaps radically to shift the way in which the agei
at the individual and social level.

What is the dominant model or image we have o
the associations that spring to mind are of decrep
nursing homes whose occupants are seen as redundant
These negative models may act as destructive, self-fulfilli
are, according to the 73-year-old retired professor
Schachter-Shalomi, part of a paradigm of ageing that nee
and transformed. The whole ageing process, he says, need
Schachter-Shalomi, who is a pioneer of interfaith dialogi
renewal, offers an alternative vision and practice of growing o
wide-ranging syntheses of modern psychology with the w
religious traditions. Underlying the vision, says Rabbi Schachte
an act of faith: a belief that 'the things of senescence that come to
age are not a lousy trick that God pulled on us. That it is goo
experience old age. That it can bring its own unique sati
(Schachter-Shalomi and Miller 1995, p.4–5).

This article outlines the vision and the practice, the concepts and ti
that Rabbi Schachter-Shalomi has developed. Their aim is to sh
experience of our latter years from what one 64-year-old friend rec

described as '
a place of jo
self-worth:
Many of
unrest. It m
that 'there
not ready
Furtherm
them bei
'retired'
meant s
from th
And
clamo
have b
betra
painl
Shal
is a

de
res
g
n
a

CHAPTER 7

Harvesting a Lifetime

Jenny Goodman

A New Paradigm of Ageing

There is something that all of us are doing all the time: growing older. How do we live this process? Will we experience old age as a burden or as a gift? As problem or as opportunity?

We are perhaps the first generation to confront issues of ageing on such a massive scale. Our extended lifespan and the population increase have combined to form an 'agewave', an unprecedentedly large number of people now entering their autumn years. It becomes crucial, then, to examine and perhaps radically to shift the way in which the ageing process is viewed, both at the individual and social level.

What is the dominant model or image we have of ageing? All too often, the associations that spring to mind are of decrepitude and senility, of nursing homes whose occupants are seen as redundant and useless to society. These negative models may act as destructive, self-fulfilling prophecies. They are, according to the 73-year-old retired professor and rabbi Zalman Schachter-Shalomi, part of a paradigm of ageing that needs to be reshaped and transformed. The whole ageing process, he says, needs healing. Rabbi Schachter-Shalomi, who is a pioneer of interfaith dialogue and spiritual renewal, offers an alternative vision and practice of growing old, based on his wide-ranging syntheses of modern psychology with the wisdom of the religious traditions. Underlying the vision, says Rabbi Schachter-Shalomi, is an act of faith: a belief that 'the things of senescence that come to us when we age are not a lousy trick that God pulled on us. That it is good for us to experience old age. That it can bring its own unique satisfactions' (Schachter-Shalomi and Miller 1995, p.4–5).

This article outlines the vision and the practice, the concepts and the tools that Rabbi Schachter-Shalomi has developed. Their aim is to shift the experience of our latter years from what one 64-year-old friend recently described as 'everybody expecting me to just wind down and disintegrate' to a place of joyful, conscious ripening, with a revitalising sense of focus and self-worth: a place from which to harvest the fruits of a lifetime.

Many older people, according to Rabbi Schachter-Shalomi, feel a kind of unrest. It may be disguised as boredom, but underneath it is a nagging sense that 'there is more I have to know, there is something I have to become. I am not ready to submit the rest of my life to diminishing physical capacity.' Furthermore, there is the worry: 'How will I spend my last years, without them being a drag on me or my loved ones?' Many older people have been 'retired' – from the French *retirer* – literally pulled away, from the work that meant something to them. They are more often asked what they have retired from than what they have retired for.

And there are aches and pains. Often these are the pains of unlived life, clamouring voices in the body saying, 'You haven't done this or that. You have broken promises to yourself.' Parts of us scream, because they have been betrayed, when we didn't follow our bliss/our purpose/our destiny. Taking painkillers to silence such regrets and longings, says Rabbi Schachter-Shalomi, is just like ripping out the cord of a ringing telephone. The message is a vital one, and it will try any which way to get through until we listen to it.

We can, says Rabbi Schachter-Shalomi, meet approaching age and decreasing physical strength with denial. Alternatively, we can 'reach for the resources that have begun to ripen, quietly, in another part of the inner garden'. We can take hold of the energy of our anxieties, and utilise it for a new unfolding, to begin what can be the most creative phase of our lives – and has indeed been recognised to be so, in other cultures and other times. The problem, of course, is that most of us lack good role models for becoming what Rabbi Schachter-Shalomi calls an 'Elder'. No one has taught us how to handle this phase of life; no one has prepared us. We need initiation into the work of Eldering.

Part of this work, says Rabbi Schachter-Shalomi, is repairing the wounds of the past. And part of it is sifting and synthesising the lessons and events of our lives, both those perceived as failures and those seen as successes, into that distillation we call wisdom. Rabbi Schachter-Shalomi calls this work 'The Ministry of Spiritual Eldering', for this is *the* season of life for doing the spiritual work of contemplation, meditation, forgiveness and letting go. It is about making what Rabbi Schachter-Shalomi calls the 'mind-moves from Ageing to Sageing' – becoming a sage, or wise one.

The Talmud tells a story that when we die we are received in the world-to-come and asked the question: 'Did you enjoy everything that the earthly world had to offer?' And if we did not, we are required to give an account of why there was some God-given pleasure of which we failed to avail ourselves.

An Elder, in Rabbi Schachter-Shalomi's sense, is 'a person who is still growing and learning, and still in pursuit of happiness, joy and pleasure. And his or her birthright to these remains intact.'

Seasons of Life

Rabbi Schachter-Shalomi invites us to visualise our lifespan in terms of the biblical seven-year cycles, and to see each cycle as one month of a calendar year. Thus our first seven years are January, from seven to fourteen – puberty – is February, and so on. Adolescence is early spring, and we reach adulthood – 21 – at the start of April. Our needs and appropriate activities will change considerably as we move through the seasons. By the end of April (age 28) we are shedding some of the aspects of youth and becoming more clearly delineated as our individual self. As we move through May and June – 35, 42 – we are often involved with establishing family, career and home. July, August and September are when we may begin our 'magnum opus', our central life's task. As we enter October, November, December, our work becomes the harvesting and wisdom-transmitting work of the Elder. In October, November and December, says Rabbi Schachter-Shalomi, we cannot afford to be addicted to habits of rushing and conquering, habits that we acquired in earlier phases of life. When we don't recognise this, and still try to do things in the old way, we become depressed or angry. One of the gifts of the autumn time is that we can be released from what Rabbi Schachter-Shalomi calls 'Commodity Time' (Monday to Friday, nine to five) into 'Organic Time' – day and night, summer and winter, harmonising our bodies to the tides and cycles of the natural world.

The Work of Spiritual Eldering

Rabbi Schachter-Shalomi teaches the contemplative art of 'Life Review', the skills for re-evaluation of the past and repair of relationships, and techniques for the harvesting of a life's experience and its transmission as wisdom into the wider world.

Of the re-evaluation work, he says that a perceived failure or painful memory can be seen as 'the grain of sand in the oyster that grows the pearl'. As we discover the hidden positive aspects in our life-story, we can in fact 'recycle discomfort, and turn it into triumph'.

There is a natural sadness that arises when we wonder what will happen to all the understanding we gained the hard way in the school of life. Will it be lost when my body is gone? One aspect of the life-force in the Eldering time is the desire to pass on what we've learnt, to contribute it into the pool of civilisation. And civilisation needs to receive the distilled wisdom of Elders as much as the Elders need to give it.

There are many ways, says Rabbi Schachter-Shalomi, in which such a harvest of wisdom can be transmitted to future generations. One of these is 'Mentoring', a direct relationship of mutual sharing and listening between an Elder and a younger person. In former times these would have been largely grandparent–grandchild relationships, which were important means for the transmission of cultural wisdom, values and traditions. (The direct parent–child relationship can never do quite the same job, partly because of the child's need to rebel at some point and therefore reject parental ideals.) Today's social mobility and nuclear family structure mean that the Elder's own grandchildren are often many miles away. But we can form mentoring relationships nonetheless, outside the bounds of the traditional extended family. These relationships are of great benefit to both people involved; the older person gains energy and vitality and the younger one gains wisdom and perspective. Much valuable oral history springs from such intergenerational friendships.

Another method of transmitting what one has learnt is the writing of 'Ethical Wills' – consciously chosen legacies of practical and philosophical insights gleaned from one's lived experience – for future generations of one's own family, or others. The deepest work of an Elder, says Rabbi Schachter-Shalomi, is 'to think in time-spans of seven generations – to plant trees that will bear fruit only after we're gone'.

To take this approach – to live freely and fully in the flow of time – requires contemplative skills. Without such skills we may find ourselves constricted, boxed in by fear of the future, stagnating rather than 'transmitting'. The contemplative and meditative techniques that suit people earlier in life may be the more active forms of meditation, but in the Elder years, says Rabbi Schachter-Shalomi, some forms of 'centering prayer' works best, such as sitting in deep silence and simple mindfulness. And not necessarily cross-legged! A hot tub is a fine and comfortable place for an Elder to practise meditation, says Rabbi Schachter-Shalomi. When insomnia troubles many older people, he points out, and they toss and turn and reach for the sleeping pills, their bodies are actually calling 'wake up' in the sense of 'become aware'! It is a pull towards the meditation that an Elder needs to be doing.

When an older person truly becomes a 'Spiritual Elder', she or he inspires honour and respect from others naturally. What might be difficult in our western culture is for Elders to allow themselves to receive that honour, to feel they deserve it. Among traditional tribal peoples this problem does not arise, because the honour that Elders receive is honour they themselves have given to others when they were younger. They know that they in turn are modelling Elderhood for those who come after them, and that the process is reciprocal; we all need to have someone we can respect and learn from. In some Native American tribes, women are revered and eligible for particularly honoured positions at the time of their menopause. What a contrast to our own youth-worshipping culture!

Facing our Mortality

In working with Elders, says Rabbi Schachter-Shalomi, it is important to recognise that people become highly anxious when they have not made peace with their own mortality. Fear of death, he points out, is 'part of the normal software for the preservation of life'. Biologically it takes the form of the adrenaline 'fight/flight' response to anything that threatens our life. Psychologically it can result in a denial of our mortality. It is like a 'programme' running in the background of consciousness, which says, 'I don't want to die, I don't want to die'. This programme is essential earlier on in life, and its life-affirming function finds a place in Halacha (Jewish Law) as a statement that 'a human life is worth more than the whole Torah [Scriptures]'. But, says Rabbi Schachter-Shalomi, if we continue to let this programme run us later in life, it can obstruct entry to the Eldering phase.

As we age, we need to be able to say, 'This programme running in me is only a programme. I am not the programme.' We need to detach ourselves from the ego's automatic response and allow the energy in the 'save your life at any cost' programme to run low. When we do this, says Rabbi Schachter-Shalomi, we can remain steadfast and do not flinch in the face of death. Beyond our fears, we can see a wonderful potential to complete and round out our life. When we stop editing out the signals of our mortality that keep coming up from our ripening and our slowing down, we can move through and beyond the frightened places. We can free the energies that were bound up in the denial of death. Paradoxically, facing the fears actually lightens our burden and liberates us for fuller living. If I can really say 'yes' to my death, then I can really say 'yes' to my life.

In his teaching, Rabbi Schachter-Shalomi has described the moment of dying thus:

> To accept life as the gift I have been given, and now to give my body to the worms and my spirit to the Universal. I flow into the Godstream not with the pain of an unlived life but with the joy of fulfillment and completion.

CHAPTER 8

Sageing in the Light of Death

Rabbi Zalman Schachter-Shalomi

Sageing is not a special gift; it is only actualising that with which we have been born, using the gift of life we already have. To accept life as the gift I have been given and now to give my body to the worms and my spirit to the Universal Spirit, I flow into the Godstream not with the pain of an unlived life but with the grateful joy of appreciated completion.

The significance of such completion is true for every person. In lecturing to hospice workers I remind them that there is a happiness that is not giddy, one that comes with being present at a good death. This kind of happiness is called in Hebrew *Ashrey*: this is the first word of the Psalter, *Ashrey Haish*, and is translated into Latin as *Beatus Vir.* Jesus used the word in the beatitudes. Among modern Beatitudes we could include: 'Blessed are the hospice workers for they hold open the gate to the Kingdom'.

However, it is not necessary to be a hospice worker to be an effective companion, being present to another person at this most significant moment in the life process. Its inspiration is compassion. Even the greatest, most fortunate and richest person will have had to undergo some suffering in their journey from birth to death: from birth trauma to colics and childhood diseases, to the stroke and the heart attack or the cancer, and that suffering calls for compassion. There is not nowadays a popularly shared place for this compassion but it has always been a foundation stone of world religions. There was in Buddhism the *Boddhisattva* who postpones his entry into the bliss-light-knowing until he has helped the last sentient being. In Judaism one speaks of *Middat HaraHhamim*, the divine attribute of mercy, the compassionate wombing of G-d, where underneath it all are the everlasting arms. In Catholicism there is the *Mater Misericordia* and the devotion to the Sacred Heart of Jesus. And in Islam the opening of the Qur'an speaks in the Name of *Allah* the Merciful, the Compassionate.

Inspired by such compassion, there are some important guidelines to bear in mind if our presence with those who die is to be helpful. First of all, it is vital to have come to terms with our own mortality and its significance – or at least to be in the process of so doing. Good deaths and difficult deaths are our teachers. For those involved regularly in this work it is important to share our experiences, our grief and our anger with others so involved. Most significant of all, and contrary to our usual habit, we recognise that there is nothing we can do for the dying to prevent their dying. So, in allowing that we cannot change the situation, our job is to hold the field for the passer. In other words our surrender helps them to surrender, and we commit to help by just being present.

If compassion lies at the heart of all religions, so in most there is an emphasis at the hour of one's death upon the *metanoia*, the turning, the 'repentance'. I don't like this last word and welcome the fact that Catholics, who take last rites so seriously, have begun to term it 'the sacrament of reconciliation'. In Judaism, even when in the old days a criminal such as a murderer was executed, he would recite the prayer, 'May my death atone for all my sins'.

Why is it that such an emphasis is put on the last moments and the reconciliation with God? When someone tells me of a parent who has passed, I usually ask, 'And were you reconciled before they died?' Blessed indeed are they who have been reconciled, for their grief work can proceed without further complications of guilt, resentment and vindictiveness. Often, after the eruption of the last anger of the dying person there is still a calming and a reconciliation with the last breaths.

The issue of reconciliation is crucial. Many are the stories of those who even through agonies reached the final reconciliation.

From a mystical point of view it makes deep sense. There is an old-new depth cosmology that speaks about such matters, and it is again breaking through, from physics and transpersonal psychology: the Anthropic principle and the Gaian hypothesis. Thank God that this has emerged from the brittle materialistic scientism of the nineteenth century.

The mystery, which needs incubation through intense contemplation as you see life and death around your own journey, can be put into these words: 'We are freed from the drama of our own life time. We can merge again with the Great One-ness at the same time as we complete it with a blessing.'

In this way we further the growth of global consciousness and advance the process of the divinisation of the planet, as Teilhard de Chardin (1964)

put it. Or, if you prefer it, in Ken Wilber's (1996) words, you further the
Atman Project.

Yet, here is the rub: we cannot further this reconciliation if we exhort,
persuade, convince, entice, impel, induce, the passer to become reconciled.
This is not the time for sectarian soul-grabbing. All we can do is hold the field
in a loving attitude where this can happen.

Here is my translation of Rabbi Heschel's (1973) sad description of 'The
Patient' in one of his Yiddish poems:

> In his bed the patient sinks midst
> Some people filled with life,
> Like a gasping fish on shore
> Of island washed by waves of sea.
>
> Silent pointers, the dials race
> As if driven by a whip.
> The old familiar time-piece wonders
> Which one of the fates will win.
>
> In the grip of the inevitable,
> The Patient lies silent, mute.
> His lips are parted supplicating.
> Wife and friends stand about him,
> He is the loneliest of them all.
>
> The dying man's heart hangs by some thread
> Of spider's web, magnetic, sweet.
> The last foothold in yet hopeful corner
> Shrinks, gets smaller, beat by beat.
>
> Past the protection of mother arms
> Life runs out, like through a sieve,
> While the eyes of the onlooking kin
> Turn to idiotic stares and whispered curse.
>
> Words and mem'ries wiped from skull,
> Only one short word remains,
> Lost in battle of death's rattle,
> Caught and fettered by vocal chord: G-d.

In *Cat's Cradle* (1963), the writer Kurt Vonnegut gives us his version of
the deathbed prayer recited by one Bokononian as his friend is dying:

God made mud, God got lonesome
So God said to some of the mud, 'Sit up!'
'See all I have made,' said God,
'the hills, the sea, the sky, the stars.'
And I was some of the mud
That got to sit up and look around.
Lucky me, lucky mud.
I, mud, sat up and saw
What a nice job God had done.
'Nice going, God!'
'Nobody but You could have done it, God!
I certainly couldn't have.'
I feel very unimportant compared to You.
The only way I can feel the least bit important
Is to think of all the mud
That didn't even get to sit up and look around.
I got so much, and most mud got so little.
'Thank you for the honor!'
Now mud lies down again
And goes to sleep.
What memories for mud to have!
What interesting other kinds of
Sitting-up mud I met!
I loved everything I saw!
'Good night.' I will go to heaven now.
I can hardly wait
To find out for certain
What my wampeter was
And who was my karass
And all the good things our karass did for you.
Amen.

I suggest finding a mantric intention for being present with the dying one. Catholics say, 'Holy Mary Mother of God, be with us failing ones now and at the hour of our death'; Muslims, '*Allahu Akbar. Allah* is greater than…'; Buddhists, *'Gate, Gate paragate, Parasamgathe – boddhi swaha – Gone, gone, way gone, gone beyond';* Jews, *'Into Thy hands I place my breath-soul. You redeem me',* and the *Sh'ma* which ends with *'ONE'.*

CHAPTER 9

Death and the Spirituality of Ageing

Penelope Wilcock

Part of our perspective as creatures of time and space is to see the world as very concrete, very solid; to understand our circumstances as given and (to a great extent) unalterable; and to use the words 'physical' and 'real' as almost synonymous.

From such a perspective, ageing and death are seen as a journey from the real to the unreal, a helpless, undesirable journey foisted upon us by the accident of being alive: unwelcome, unpleasant, and best ignored for as long as possible.

In our age, the cults of youth and of hardness dominate our thinking — thinness, toughness, speed, survival, athleticism, muscularity — all that is cutting, all that is abrasive, all that succeeds. Softness, fatness, slowness, quietness, hesitancy — what use has the modern world for these?

In such an age, to grow old is to have all we have succeeded in evading outwit us and defeat us at last. The collapse and dissolution of the physical form; the surrender of youth and hardness: in our day no wisdom prepares us for the different perspective on reality which might enable us to live at peace with the challenge of this journey.

But it need not be so. There are other perspectives, there are paths of peace. In our day the Church would do the world a great kindness if, instead of being seduced by the fears and aspirations which are the legacy of rationalism and materialism, it could open again the crumbled and overgrown ways of the spiritual life, so that an increasingly ageing population might find dignity, tranquillity and hope, in growing old.

The Emergence of the Spiritual Self

Where is the soul?

Christianity grows out of Judaism. In Hebrew, the word for the spirit – *ruach* – is the same word as that used for 'wind' or 'breath'. Before the soph- istication of life-support machines and diagnoses of brain death, a person was alive as long as they breathed. 'Life and breath' rolled into one phrase. Thus the spirit was the life of the person, the radiance, the wholeness, the self, apparent in every part, but limited to no particular system. The soul is not, as we are now sometimes inclined to assume, a part of brain function. The soul is not localised in the central nervous system. The soul is greater, deeper, underlying and pre-existing all bodily systems and bodily development.

With a firm understanding of this, an understanding that living beings are – in their core, their root, their foundation – *spiritual*, then we shall be well placed to find a different understanding of what happens when the body grows old.

Physics and theology are twin disciplines, exploring from different angles the same truth. The physical deterioration that is observable in the world of space and time is inseparable from the strengthening of the soul as it shakes loose from its bonds.

Water is determined by two tendencies: the tendency of itself towards roundness, and the tendency of gravity to elongate it by its down-pulling force. So water moves forever in vortexes and spirals, as the lengthening of gravity interacts with its own sphericality in determining the patterns of its motion.

Similarly, the pattern and path of the self is determined by the interaction of the laws of physics ('dust to dust') with the laws of spirit, by which our habits of mind strengthen and develop the soul until it finds its moment to slip free of the physical confines of earthiness. The form of a human self grows out of the interplay of the continual drawing of Spirit upon the being of earth. Earth has its own roundness, its own self-containedness, but spirit irresistibly yearns towards Spirit. Found in flesh, earthed and yet alien, it is forever called home to something beyond, half-remembered, half-glimpsed.

Planting a potato is the beginning of a life journey. The new potato plant begins inside the being of the seed potato, but gradually puts forth shoots and is drawn up out of earth towards air and light. In the process, the life of the seed potato is used up. When the gardener digs up the new potatoes, the old seed potato can be found not far away, a used and finished old sac whose time has gone.

As youngsters, we are all of a piece with our bodies, that is what our innocence is. Not separated out yet into the knowledge of good and evil, our bliss and desire as newborns are milk and sleep and being held. But in time our spirits grow up out of our earthiness toward the air and light of the spirit. That's why more old people go to church; they are no longer enmeshed in the physicality of getting and having, sex and busyness and toil. The new shoot of their souls is journeying away from that towards the light. And as it journeys away, so it gradually uses up the store of life that God breathed into the seed part of the whole being; so the physical part shrivels and diminishes as the soul is strengthened and set free. This is not to understand that old people are more spiritual than babies, or that life begins as matter and the soul comes into it only later. On the contrary, all matter is made by God, and as God is Spirit, it follows that matter is innately spiritual and innately wise. The very first impulse of new life is spiritual. But at first the matter and the spirit are undivided, all of a piece. It is the soul's yearning towards God that draws it slowly away from earthiness. Ageing is the soul leaving the body behind.

In speaking of this spiritual journey as a passage up towards the light, it should not be understood that the earthy world of the body is lower or lesser; God makes everything beautiful in its time, and the body has the right dignity and holiness of earth while the spirit finds its proper home in the freedom of light and eternity, no longer shackled by its small house of space and time.

Identity and Personhood

A self is a world, a microcosm. Its oneness is not monochrome but flames with richness of variety. Different modes of being, different aspects of self, are held together in equilibrium in a well person. Under pressure of stress, or dementia, or misery, or drug treatment, sometimes the dance of being falters and loses its rhythm, the integrity of personality is lost, and selfhood splinters, resulting in confusion, misplaced and inappropriate behaviour, and loss of confidence. Sometimes obsessiveness or neurosis manifest the severe anxiety that results from this sense of losing the self. A self is not a thing but a balancing, a gathering, an interacting: the vertigo of a self losing its balance is terrifying, because its balance is what makes it a self. Then who is terrified by the stumbling, the disintegration of the self? It is the soul who is terrified, frightened of being cast out of its earthy home, afraid to throw caution to the winds and seek its eternal home in God.

The self is found, created and shaped, through relationship: interaction with other human beings, with the created world in all its richness and possibility, and with the inner reality of our spiritual understanding – whatever, for us, is meant by God.

In old age, much of what created our sense of self changes. Who we were as a lover, a partner, is lost as sexual capacity diminishes and the partner is lost through death or other partings of the ways. Sometimes, coming to terms with the diminishing of sexual capacity, the loss of firmness and physical elasticity, the new determination of men's hair to grow on the head no longer, but vigorously out of the nose, and in women to sprout as a luxuriant beard and moustache – these changes, along with the softness, the stiffness, the fatness that come, are a humiliation never to be underestimated. Most of us are too proud to discuss it. And the loss of a partner is a bitter grief. The increasing instability of sexual partnerships inevitably heightens the anxiety associated with increased vulnerability and the loss of sexual attractiveness.

Who we were as a worker, a person of strength, must also change. The ferocious control which some elderly people exert over their sphere of influence in the church – the choir, the taking of the collection, the flower arranging – in part arises from redundancy in the world of work. No one wants to be a has-been, no longer consulted, no longer useful, no longer needed, out of date.

Who we were as a provider changes too. Children move away, and visit seldom, busy with their own lives.

These are not easy changes. They bring with them inevitably a fearful question, 'Who am I, now?' The roles of lover, partner, worker and provider take so much time, so much concentration, so much energy; little wonder if in the middle years we found no time to dream, to meditate, to grow in wisdom. In our society, which places so much emphasis on sex and work, and which has little clear concept of or desire for wisdom, growing old is a bleak prospect, even for the bravest and most loved.

Strengthening the Sense of Self

The task of dying is a tremendous event. To see dying as no more than what we call the end of life is to miss life's most intoxicating spiritual ascent: for this is not the end of anything; it is the approach to God, the beginning, the chance at last to behold life's mystery as a friend. A person needs to be in good shape to die well. It is of tremendous importance, as the soul approaches death, that the community of love surround the preparing soul and strengthen her with nourishment for the journey.

The soul is nourished by what God is, for she is made in God's image. God is spirit, light, truth, love, gentleness, laughter, strength, faithfulness, glory: and with all these things must the soul be nourished to make the great ascent to the holy ground of God's dwelling.

But as old age increases, so often the soul is not nourished by these gifts of love from the community. The changes in identity and role as the body ages bring with them uncertainty, uncomfortable vulnerability and a need for reassurance. Sometimes outright fear further diminishes the sense of con-fidence. Con-fidence: it means 'with faith'. Fear decreases a person's ability to die with faith. It is love that casts out fear. In old age there are so many things to be afraid of: fear of the darkness under whose cover muggers and burglars may lurk; fear of physical aggression from others; fear of being inadequate in responding to changing ways of technology; fear of crossing the road in the busy traffic; fear of falling; fear of looking foolish because of deafness or impaired vision; fear of fumbling the change on the bus and incurring the impatience of the harassed driver. Fear that all this humiliation is an indication of worthlessness.

Trying to help, voluntary workers, shop assistants, nurses 'deal with', 'handle', the elderly person briskly, kindly, not meaning to patronise, but the message is clear. Now no longer 'madam', no longer 'sir'; now 'dear'. An old dear. Dear is removed by one letter from 'dead'.

Not 'dear', not dead! A person, alive, suffering – it's MEEEEEEEE!

As we age, how desperately we need as a gift what we can no longer earn by our status as worker, as partner, as lover: friendship that never patronises, that has time to listen, that does not always take us seriously but lets us laugh. Fun. We still need to have fun when we are old. Oh the dignity, the peace of being loved. Whatever else old age may bring, let it bring friendship.

I have seen many deaths, but there is one among them all that haunts me. Evelyn was her name, and she lived in a bed in a small, cosy room in the eaves of a nursing home. Nobody visited her. Nobody sat with her. The staff came from time to time to feed her, or change her soiled bedlinen, nothing else. There was no music in her room, nothing to help the hours pass. Entering her room, the stench of bad flesh was appalling. She had had operations to re-place her hip joints. However successful they may once have been, now they were wounds with wires protruding. The base of her spine was afflicted with an ugly, necrotic bedsore. She showed no sign of life or response, except that when we approached the bed to turn or change her, as soon as she was aware of our presence she would begin to scream. She had oozing diarrhoea, which aggravated the condition of the bedsore. On the last night of Evelyn's life, I was on night duty. It was customary to leave her alone, but I wanted to sit with her. And I stayed with her through the small hours of that last night, watching at her bedside, as the rasping labour of breathing signalled the coming end. Her tongue, dry and brown, hung out of her mouth, her lips were parched and cracked. In that nursing home there was no provision but a commode, a roll of toilet tissue and a washing-up bowl with a flannel. There had been nothing else to ease her discomfort or keep infection at bay. The artificial saliva spray, the pink mouth sponges, the breathing mattresses, the volunteer to sit at the bedside that would have been hers in a hospice were unheard of in the place where Evelyn ended her days. There was just me, watching and praying beside her, doing what I could to moisten her poor mouth with the toilet tissue dipped in water from the sink. Then, as morning drew near, five o'clock came and I had to leave her, go down to the kitchen to prepare the porridge, the cornflakes, the marmalade sandwiches, for the other forsaken creatures who, behind their own closed doors, shared this building that nobody could have called home. And eventually, when we could spare a moment to check her, she was dead.

This death haunts me still. O God, let it not be like that for me! All that I might say of positive encouragement about the spirituality of old age and dying dies on my lips when I confront this ghoulish icon of contemporary spirituality, the modern way to die. And when I remind myself that it doesn't have to be like that, it brings small comfort, because I know that Evelyn was helpless: she had found, willingly or not, the severest way of all, the way of the Christ: of vulnerability and helplessness that gives the rest of us an opportunity of mercy. Which we may, or may not, take.

So, part of the spirituality of ageing and death is a revealing of God's agenda, often masked till now in the illusions of strength and sex: God's agenda that we should love one another; that we should learn to be vulnerable and to trust. And that we should learn to have mercy.

The gift of life is for acquiring wisdom and compassion. The learning curve accelerates sharply here. To those who are growing old, those of us who will one day also be old can offer the gift of love; affirmation of personhood; gentleness; the grace of patience and of understanding; the grace of listening and waiting for someone slower than our own pace to take their time. If it does nothing else it will be good practice; for plenty of self-effacement, plenty of patience, will be required of us as we grow old.

And as we offer the gift of love, the miracle happens. We cannot take all the aches and pains and confusion away (though more can be done to help there than we often suppose), but we can lift the anxiety, and the loneliness, and make life feel less frightening by being there.

Habit Energy

I shall be always grateful to the Buddhist teacher, Thich Nhat Hanh, for creating the phrase 'habit energy', because in old age it is such a powerful thing.

The popular misconception is that in old age and in dying we lose more and more, become less and less like ourselves, whereas in fact the reverse is true. Even in those dementias where loved ones feel they have been bereaved even while the body lives; even when the physical deterioration is so severe that friends and relatives say 'she's no longer herself; that's not her any more' – even in such situations the soul shines through, and doggedly, inevitably, goes on creating a self out of whatever potential remains.

And the self that is created depends on habit energy. Habit energy is one of the most powerful forces in our lives, and one of the most precious spiritual tools we have. Its power can be a vital asset in sickness, in old age, in dying. Yet though the understanding of it is commonplace, the valuing of it as a potent, wonderful gift is rare enough.

Habit energy is no more than 'you can't teach an old dog new tricks' or 'a journey of a thousand miles begins with the first step'. It is the solid rock hardened through the years of attitudes of mind; ways of thinking, speaking and acting.

A self-disciplined life will lay down patterns of habit that will over the years accumulate formative energy, shaping us physically, mentally and spiritually, so that when youth energy is gone, that once enabled us to straighten up out of chaotic living again and again, we shall have invested in habits of mind that create a positive energy to sustain us in the inevitable complex of adversities (bereavements, physical vulnerability and frailty etc.) arriving with our old age.

The habit energy of a disciplined life is formed out of paying constant, regular attention to the following things:

- prayer and meditation, of any form consistent with the ideology of the individual

- physical health, well-being and fitness, in terms of diet, exercise, fresh air, light, rest and moderation

- pursuing some form of work, requiring the development of stamina and application

- self-respect expressed in dress and posture, leisure interests and treats

- positive thinking expressed in tolerance, courtesy and friendliness

- responsible handling of finance with an emphasis on the generosity that affirms faith in providence and the goodness of life

- a commitment to self-education in spiritual development and in understanding of the workings of mind, soul and body

- taking responsibility for one's own life, and refusing to regard oneself as the victim of circumstance or misfortune.

Over a lifetime of practising self-disciplined living, the old dog that cannot be taught new tricks can rest upon the immovable rock of habit, can be carried along by the inevitable momentum of habit, once the vitality of youth begins to wane.

It is not the case that the world is the way it is and we are the helpless victims of the environment in which we find ourselves. Our experience of our world largely depends upon our individual perspective, and that in turn is determined by our own attitudes of mind. It is possible for us *literally* to change our world by choosing to look at it from a different perspective, and then strengthening our new perspective with habit.

Even on the greater scale this is true. Who would have believed, 50 years ago, that human beings could alter the weather? And yet by the faithful daily habits of the western world in following the dictates of market-place values at the expense of environmental interest, we have succeeded in changing our climate beyond saving. If we can do this, by combined and sustained habits of choice, what else may we not achieve, for good or ill, by the astonishing power of choice and habit?

No one should underestimate the power of the human spirit, made as it is in the image of God who is creator, to affect and transform our experience of reality. Life does not just happen to us, we are not its helpless victims; our circumstances are opportunities out of which we may shape the life we choose. Acquiring the habit of meeting life's opportunities with a loving, non-judgemental spirit, an attitude of gratitude for grace given and trust in God's providence, will transform our reality by transforming our perception. Acquiring habits of spiritual light literally changes the world, since we know the world only through our perspective, see it only from our point of view. As these habits of mind are strengthened by repetition, gradually they form the solidity of many layers, and begin to support us. The younger we begin to form new perspectives, the less of the old we have to dismantle and diminish, and the longer we have to form a bulwark of habit energy to carry us through difficult times. But anyone at any moment can choose to leave negativity behind and chance new perspectives of love and hope; when we do that, the whole universe works together with us for good, adding the strength of everything to our own; for love is what we were made for, love is the lifeblood of the cosmos.

In the formation of habit energy, perhaps the most uplifting and strengthening habit to acquire is that of living in the light of something greater than ourselves. Freedom and peace are found by trusting to an intelligence beyond ourselves, resting in a goodness that underlies everything, flowing with the stream of life that is for everyone.

When faith in God is not part of an individual's understanding, still one is helped by being lifted beyond the self. This can be expressed in commitment to an ideological movement, or to the community. It can be to a discipline or an interest such as art or gardening or dance or archaeology or politics; but if there is *anything* that interests one more than oneself, a consuming passion to take us beyond ourselves, a light of something above and beyond us by which we may live, then the experience of growing older and approaching death is less terrifying than if our interests and attention are focused narrowly within the self.

Living, Dying, Ageing and Community

The religions and philosophies of the world vary in their moral structure, except that the grounding for moral structure is almost invariably conceived in community.

Whether it is the Christian teaching of loving the brotherhood and the neighbour, or the Jewish teaching of the People of God, or the Hindu concept of Karma and caste, the Buddhist concepts of the Dharma and the Sangha, or the atheist ideology of humanism, the moral universe has more in it than just me. Its aspirations are compassion and respect, reverence for life; and it frowns upon selfishness, indifference and exploitation.

In our day, somehow attention has been diverted from the building up of community to quite extreme forms of autonomous individualism. The prevalence of television; distance communication of all sorts (from e-mail to the use of telephone shopping); the erosion of public transport and the prevalence of the car; the shift in emphasis to small family homes housing nuclear families moved away from their roots; the shift from small local shops to big out-of-town one-stop-shop stores: all these have eroded community at the same time as enhancing choice and possibility for the individual. The comfort of central heating and the affordability of electrical goods has been welcome; but gone are the days when freezing bedrooms drove the family together to share the warmth of the living room fire. Parents fear for their children's safety in the anonymous societies of towns infested with traffic.

Today's children often occupy their leisure hours alone in centrally heated bedrooms, entertained by their own television, their own computer, their own music system. And increasingly, just as their parents' marriages fail, leaving single-parent households with the only adult out at work, so the elderly must struggle alone, often hundreds of miles away from their dispersed families. Then when the frailties of old age make living alone impossible, the move to a nursing home is made; and the last months or years of life are often spent sitting in a chair in a solitary room, too blind and deaf to enjoy the television, too confused to learn or influence a new environment. Care staff cost money, so no one has time to chat or stay awhile. The highlights of the day are the meals.

We have enhanced the physical comforts and convenience of our lives phenomenally: and this is a tremendous blessing, except for its cost to the ecological environment and the price we pay in the most profound human loneliness.

In every challenge of life, in all fear or grief or adversity, in all pain or distress, and most of all when the spectre of death comes terrifyingly near, we need a friend. We need companionship. Love. This is not the icing on the cake when all other provisions are in place; this is the most fundamental human need, without which all creature comforts bring scant joy, and with which we can face the worst with courage.

Especially for the elderly, facing the loss of one after another of their friends, facing the loneliness of the task of growing old, shaking loose the trappings of earth and looking eternity in the face, the ordinary familiarity of friendship, the reassurance of being loved, is necessary above all else. Even pain and physical aches and troubles diminish when one is loved.

If the time comes to accept the necessity for residential care, that heart-rending wrench of leaving one's home is softened by a continuation of friends' visits and letters and conversation.

In considering the spirituality of ageing and death, the first priority beyond all others turns out to be the same priority as for all the rest of life: 'Love your neighbour as yourself'.

Just as when we were children, learning to know the world; just as when we were young adults, trying to make a home, raise a family, find a job; just as when mid-life crisis struck; just as in all the horrors of redundancy and piles and middle-aged spread, teenage spots and broken dates, failed exams and driving tests and marriages, it was the ones who loved us who kept us sane: so in our old age and in our dying, it is love which brings peace and sees us through.

God who made us, made us to need one another, and to belong together. God in the discipline of His mercy makes loneliness miserable. The challenge of our day turns out to have changed little in 2000 years: Love your neighbour as yourself ... And who is my neighbour?

CHAPTER 10

The Memory Box

Jackie Treetops

The project was launched in 1995 by 'Faith in Elderly People', an inter-church group based in Leeds concerned with the spiritual needs of older people. This group had itself come into being as a consequence of the 'Faith in Leeds' process which had studied the social needs of the city to which the churches might make a significant response.

The original idea for the Memory Box came from hearing on the radio in 1993 about the launch of the Barnado's 'Memory Store' for the children of families in which one parent or both parents were affected with HIV/AIDS. Physically, this Memory Store is a sturdy yellow box the size of an attaché case. Its purpose is described thus:

> The unique box can be used to store treasured mementoes, such as a favourite bedtime storybook, baby's first tooth, a lock of hair, letters, photos, important documents, a video of the family together and a tape recording of the parent's voice. (Barnado's 1993)

The Memory Store in this way can help any family preserve their identity. Children find out about themselves directly from their parents. Barnado's have developed its use especially with families where a parent is terminally ill, or for children coming into care and moving from one placement to another. A core of significant memories and mementoes is kept intact until the child is of age to add their own mementoes or to explore their own roots.

The Faith in Leeds Memory Box is described below. It too is designed to move on with a person, through the changes of home and life, a personal depository for those mementoes that are held dear to oneself. Collecting for it can begin at any age, in childhood years, the teens, middle or old age. The Memory Box is especially useful as one grows older and may need to move to smaller accommodation, or into sheltered housing, residential or nursing care. Retirement is often a time of reflection and change of lifestyle. Making a

Memory Box and sorting one out at this stage of life can be an invaluable exercise.

Why a Memory Box?

The purpose of the Memory Box is to stimulate the memory as we get older. Each one of us carries a store of memories, a living memory box. Everything we experience in life is recorded, be it through sight, sound, taste, smell or touch. At a later date it is possible to recall with pleasure (and sometimes pain) some of that past experience.

A Memory Box can help us sustain our unique personhood, for our identity is closely related to all that we have done and been. In old age – and especially when there is the onset of dementia – childhood memories may become vivid whilst recent memories turn more hazy. To help retain our identity and our 'spirit', a Memory Box, containing meaningful 'memory joggers', personal items and photographs, can be a source of pleasure and encouragement as we make the journey into old age. The Memory Box can be explored many times. Each item will hold a memory that can be revisited time and time again (Treetops 1992).

Unpacking and handling a treasured object can transport a person from the four walls of a nursing home to a place rich in memory. Jack, an older person with dementia, sits blankly looking at a television screen. His daughter Helen comes to visit. 'Hello,' she says, but Jack continues to stare. Helen gets out Jack's Memory Box and helps him unpack it. She passes him an old treasured cricket ball. He holds it in his gnarled arthritic hands, then rolls it between his palms. As he holds the ball, he remembers, his face lights up and his talk becomes animated. The touch and feel of the ball has brought back a happy memory.

Elsie, who is nearly 90, takes a palm cross out of her box. She strokes it and begins to unwrap a whole chapter of her life as a child: going to church, receiving a palm cross, Sunday School and the songs she sang, even the vicar. Happy memories, not only valuable to Elsie herself but fascinating to the listener and providing welcome pointers for conversation. A brief respite from the present moment of being bedridden, confused and paralysed, and providing a happy sojourn. Also, a little bit of history, more understanding of the person, and potential for a developing relationship. To those who have a religious faith, putting together a Memory Box, sorting it and using it can become a spiritual reflection, reminding the person of where God has been and still is at work in their life (Treetops 1996).

Type of Box Needed

A box roughly 12 inches by 9 by 15 is ideal. It needs to be strong and robust, easy to store. Any tough cardboard box will do, such as that produced by Barnado's (though theirs is rather expensive). Inside it has matching folders for paper memories and little drawers for the storage of small objects, such as those mentioned above, and there is also included a Memory Book in which to record in written form a child's own memories. Memory Stores can be purchased from the head office of Barnado's in Ilford.

Some people may prefer a metal box, available from most DIY stores at a reasonable price, or even a small suitcase. Such receptacles can be decorated externally to the owner's taste! Some folk have said that they would need a large removal van! Their work of reflection and sorting has obviously yet to be done. Some people may wish to have a locking box or bag – it all depends what you want to put in it.

What to Put in the Box

What to put in the box depends entirely on the individual. It may be just one object or photo, or a whole range of things. Remember that experiences memorised by the brain are not only visually based. Photos and diaries may be invaluable reminders, but a perfume from one's courting days or even the distinctive smell of two-stroke engine oil can be very evocative, as can the scent of a particular flower or of bread baking. Our sense of smell is very powerful and can give immediate entry into experiences from the distant past. Cherished mementoes or objects that can be touched and held, such as a teddy bear or a rag doll, a packet of seeds, a candle to be lit, a favourite silk scarf or piece of jewellery – all these can be very real memory prompts. Music or an old film on video also act as powerful memory joggers.

One object that has recently become such a cue for residents in a Leeds residential home is a pebble. In preparation for a Lent group session I was taking with some of the residents, I put some pebbles, of a size that fit comfortably into the palm of one's hand, into the freezer. We sat around a table and I passed a little basket containing them round the group. The ladies jumped when they took them, for they were very cold, and kept changing them from hand to hand. I asked them to hold their pebbles tight in one hand and told them that sometimes when we want to pray we feel cold like those pebbles, so I asked them to hold them all the time to see what would happen. I asked them how they prayed; they all shared a lot, and I learned a lot! At the end of the session I asked how their stones felt, and their answers were 'it's hot', 'warm', 'nice'. I said, 'That's what God does for us when we pray: he surrounds us with love, holds us in his hand and makes us warm and lovely'. I was later told by a member of staff that they had put their stones in their bedrooms, not to be moved. Some still hold their stone when they say their prayers. Not yet an item in a Memory Box, but the principle is the same and it certainly underlines the evocative power of touch.

However, we need to be aware that some of the items an older person selects for their Memory Box may open the door into past pain. Sad memories may be awakened, especially if one is in a vulnerable situation of change or loss such as illness, bereavement or moving home. A photograph of a dead spouse or child may bring back the grief and sadness – but sadness is part of life as much as joy, and reflection may help the healing process.

The person making up their own Memory Box must themselves decide what to put in. It is their Memory Box. Of course, in a situation where someone has been severely disabled, perhaps by a stroke, it is helpful for a friend or relative to bring in some mementoes from the person's home. The older person's choice can be painful sometimes for the family looking on. Martha was in her eighties. Her first husband had died nearly 20 years back, her second husband three years ago. Martha's adult children were distressed that she did not put in her box a single photo or memento of her first husband, their father.

Some people may well wish to put in their box things that are confidential. This needs to be respected, though they would be well advised to label them as such. In making one's selection it is worth asking the question: when I am dead what effect will this box have on those who find it? Will its contents cause offence and bitterness, or joy or understanding or shock? Will anyone feel hurt or left out? However, in the end the contents of the Memory Box remain the outcome of a person's own reflection and choice.

How to Use the Memory Box

The Memory Box can be used as a treasure chest of past experience, especially those happy times. Jessie, unable to walk unaided, loved to sit and listen to a tape of Richard Tauber singing. The music took her back to her courting days, to queuing outside the theatre, standing on the steps, and then the joy of having a seat and listening to this wonderful singer, an inspiration from her youth.

Rita, in her early sixties and recently retired, found great pleasure and satisfaction in gathering together mementoes, letters and photos for her

Memory Box. It made her stop and think about life. To reflect on where she had been, the journey she had made in life, the things to be thankful for, her children, work and personal faith. It led her also to reconcile a relationship that had caused much pain and hurt in the past. For Rita, making a Memory Box was a very real, creative and redemptive work.

Those suffering with dementia may find their favourite music and mementoes a great comfort, or even the smell of a flower evocative, but may find it very hard to deal with sad or painful memories. Healing of past hurts is unlikely to take place in the later stages of dementia. If a person with dementia has in their box a photo or other object that disturbs them, we should not prevent them from exploring the memory but rather make sure that we have plenty of time to listen and to stay with them in the pain. Sensitivity and caution are needed. Indeed, whenever you are sharing or exploring a Memory Box with anyone make sure that you have ample time and space to go through the joys and the pain with them, to hear their feelings, and to support, enable and encourage.

The value of group reminiscence work has long been recognised by the professional carers: doctors, nurses, social workers and care assistants. It encourages older people to converse with one another and can be both stimulating and relaxing (Osborne 1993). The Memory Box differs from group reminiscence work (be that through drama, music or a communal box of mementoes for handling) in that each Memory Box is unique to its individual owner.

A Memory Box can of course be used to share with others of a similar age, to remember together, to talk about past time and to trigger others in similar ways, but each box remains personal to the individual. No one should be pushed into sharing it in a group. Sharing the contents with a professional carer or a friend may also show the riches of all that person has been and is. The Memory Box can be a powerful means of deepening relationships and understanding with family, friends and carers, both private and professional.

Another possible shared use is with a child. It may be one's grandchild or even a child from a local school. Such sharing can be fascinating and very effective in bringing the older and younger generations together, in sharing a sense of history and in increasing awareness and valuing of the older person in the community. There have been recent press reports of nursery schools being established within the premises of care homes and the fertile links that this enables (Wilce 1996). A very useful handbook to facilitate such intergenerational work has been produced by Age Exchange, an organisation dealing with reminiscence and older people (Schweitzer 1993).

Evaluation

Adult or young, we are all unique and precious. Barnado's, the forerunners in making a specific Memory Store, have in a very concrete way found a means to value the individual. It has proved very successful and has been employed in many different situations. At present they are engaged in its updating and soon it will be available at a less expensive price.

Use of the Memory Box over the past three years has served to underline certain factors if best value is to be received. For many generations people have collected photographs of their family and friends and the places they have visited. All Memory Stores and Boxes are likely to contain such photos. However, if a person should become confused, pictorial or written memories may be of little value in themselves if they are not clearly labelled and people and places identified, so that carers can prompt the memory where necessary. It would indeed be useful to have a little index in the Memory Box recording why one has included each item, its associations, as well perhaps as a list of favourite foods, places and flowers. Some people will love porridge and hate scrambled egg, and will not want an unpleasant memory jog each morning!

In Scotland, the Stirling Dementia Services Development Centre has developed a Memory Book technique for use with those in residential care and their families. It enables the recording of a life history and can influence care plans and improve a person's life in a care home (Murphy 1994). This is a useful tool and could be used alongside gathering mementoes for the Memory Box for those going into (or already in) residential or nursing care. It would be of enormous help if every new resident were to come complete with Memory Box and/or Memory Book, willing to share with carers something of what they have valued in their lives.

Those people whom Faith in Elderly People have enabled to make their own Memory Box have found it a satisfying and helpful activity. In later life, hopefully, it will help them to retain their unique identity. The making of Memory Boxes has engendered such a positive response, not only reflective but therapeutic, that Faith in Elderly People has now employed a project worker to develop this work, emphasising especially mementoes that trigger the senses. Group reminiscence is now being done in a limited way with people from other cultures, and Faith in Elderly People has started to explore the possibility of using the Memory Box with those belonging to other faiths and ethnic groups. This seems particularly important for those who may have lived their youth in a hot, colourful environment, full of a sense of community and its own mystique, which it is vital they do not lose in their new situation.

To the reader of this article, two final questions. What would you put in your Memory Box? And perhaps more importantly, when do you intend starting it?

CHAPTER 11

Worshipping with those who have Dementia

Margaret Goodall

'Are thy wonders known in the darkness, or thy saving help in the Land of Forgetfulness.' (Psalm 88:12 RSV)

Introduction

Six years ago I made my first visit to Westbury, a Methodist Home for the Aged for those with dementia, as its new part-time Chaplain. I knew very little about dementia, except for what I had learned from information published by the Alzheimer's Disease Society. My first encounter with dementia was still a shock as I could not see what I could do to minister to the residents. Some of them had had a church background in mainstream denominations, while for others their only contact with the Church was through 'rites of passage' or school assembly.

During regular visiting I came to know the residents as individuals, full of character, rather than the 'empty vessels' I had first feared. The content of the service slot, at 2.30pm each Sunday afternoon for half an hour, was as varied as the people who took turns to lead it and, as I learnt more about the needs of these special people with dementia, I became aware that we had to do more than offer our thoughts, prayers and sympathy: we had to offer 'appropriate care'.

Kitwood and Bredin (1992) describe appropriate care as 'that which respects and honours personhood and provides increasing interpersonal compensation and reassurance as individual powers fail' (p.44). Our challenge was to use this model of care as we developed worship within the Home. What follows is an account of how we did this at Westbury.

The Framework

In the Free Church tradition, leaders of worship are encouraged to use variety in their choice of hymns and prayers, in order to engage the imagination of the congregation and give life to the worship. At Westbury the opposite seems to be true. We have come to realise that what seems to be needed is consistency and repetition, which then becomes a familiar framework for this special time together. Our liturgy needed 'to follow a sufficiently familiar pattern for people to be set free from thinking about what to say or do next in order to pray the liturgy and allow themselves to be absorbed by it' (Perham 1984, p.19).

There has to be a relaxed atmosphere, but one which is 'held' so that people know that someone else is responsible for what is happening. It should not be allowed to disintegrate into chaos, despite interruptions and unexpected happenings. Someone has to be in charge and be able to pull together the threads of whatever is presented, so that all is brought into the worship of the people where every response is accepted without judgement. There needs to be a pattern, but with enough flexibility to cope with the unexpected. It is an event set in the context of the Home, an event which includes the time, the place, the people, and the Christian story within the event.

The Time

We have found that the week at Westbury is given shape by holding the service on a Sunday afternoon. For those who were used to attending church it would not make sense to hold it on any other day; Sunday and church go together. When one lady asked if she had brought her coat to church today and another asked when the collection was going to be taken, I felt that we were enabling connections to be made. We came to realise that the service we held on a Sunday could reinforce memory cues brought to light by the daily exploring of the residents' own 'life story' with the staff (Goldsmith 1996, p.86). This is valuable for the individual, as it has been found that it fosters a feeling of well-being, and for the staff, who see the person in a different light. This seems to be because we have more information with which to develop a deeper appreciation of the resident: 'Knowledge of the narrative of the other is knowledge of the other. I think it is impossible to communicate with clients if the life story is unknown' (Goldsmith 1996, p.88).

Alison Froggatt (Froggatt and Shamy 1992, p.18) writes of one person with the beginnings of dementia asking, 'What will happen to my faith when I can no longer remember?'(p.18) By our worship we had enabled these ladies to cue into their memories of times past when they had attended church and they seemed to grow through the reliving of past events brought into the present. For those who did not regularly attend church but in the past had enjoyed 'Songs of Praise' or 'Sunday Half Hour', memories may be strong enough to link the service to a special day. We have tried to hold services on other days, but these have often caused confusion, especially if the time of day was also changed; this underlined the importance of consistency, pattern and repetition.

The Place

The setting for service at Westbury is the entrance lounge. This may not seem an ideal place for a service as chairs are put out in short rows, visitors come and go through the front doors and there is a lift at one side giving access to the upper floor! However, it does have the advantage of being an open space where people feel able to come and go during the service. Residents can move about freely, which is advantageous to those who are only able to join us for a short while because of the nature of their dementia. Others stay but then go when they have had enough! In addition we gain members of the congregation from 'passers by' who decide to stop and join in for a while. Members of staff and visitors who come to the service help by being there to support and encourage the residents. I am also part of the setting so I wear formal clothes (and a cassock when we share the Communion service) as cues to past memories which can be accessed through the visual.

The People

In this way we began to organise the time and the place, but the form of the service needed great thought. It may be a Methodist Home, but there are people there from all denominations as well as those who have little or no experience of 'church'. So a non-denominational service was devised. We set the scene for worship by remembering where we are and why we are together. The leader says, 'My name is ... and we have come together this afternoon, Sunday [date], at Westbury to worship God'.

At the beginning of our time of worship we use a liturgy based on one from the Iona Community *Worship Book* (1989):

LEADER: O give thanks to the Lord for he is good.

ALL: His mercy endures for ever.

LEADER: In the beginning when it was very dark God said, 'Let there be light'.

ALL: And there was light.

(The symbol of light, a candle, is placed on the empty table and lit.)

LEADER: In the beginning, when it was very quiet, The Word was with God.

ALL: And The Word was God.

(The symbol of The Word, a Bible, is opened and placed on the table.)

LEADER: When the time was right God sent His Son.

ALL: He came among us, and was one of us.

(The symbol of the Son, a cross, is placed on the table.)

We believed that it was important to make use of signs and symbols that would either cue in memories of other services the residents had attended or feed some aspect of their spiritual lives. They are important as ways into the imagination and memory; in fact, 'Not to use symbols ... in liturgy ... is to fight with one hand tied behind one's back' (Thiselton 1986, p.23).

While the candle is being lit the silence is full of meaning, perhaps with the rekindling memories of special occasions such as church, birthdays, Christmas or candlelit suppers, or as a focus to still the mind. The Bible and the wooden cross are symbols common to most Christians so can unite us in worship whatever our tradition. We cannot know all the images that may come to mind on seeing these symbols, as 'Symbols can express not only faith but also wistful memories of lost faith' (Stevenson 1981, p.22).

We wondered how a set service would be received and whether including responses was perhaps asking too much of the residents. The service had come to have a regular pattern but I still had my doubts about the appropriateness of the responses for the residents until the occasion I used a reading from Genesis in another part of the service. The reading included the words, 'And God said, "Let there be light"', and before I could continue, the residents had responded with, 'And there was light'! I had thought that it was the visitors and staff who said the responses but this occasion proved me wrong as they would have realised that words were used in another context. The residents had learnt the words of the responses: they had made the service their own.

Prayers are said thanking God for his love to us, confessing our sins and receiving God's forgiveness. It has been said to me that confession and absolution are out of place in worship with those with dementia, but I believe that as humans we all have the need to say that we are sorry and hear that we are forgiven. Saying the confession together may remove some of the sense of isolation and enable a feeling of community, for 'Faith ... is strengthened by contact with the faith of others' (Simkins 1995, p.8). In this respect those with dementia are no different from anyone else: the service is one of the few occasions when all are together and worship 'can have an important role in helping to create an experience of true community' (Methodist Conference Commission on Worship 1988, p.30).

We follow this by saying the Lord's Prayer together. The words of this can often be retrieved even when other speech is lost, buried deep in early memory. I have learnt that prayers said together have to be repeated very slowly and, contrary to usual practice, with eyes open. If you watch those with dementia in a service very few of them close their eyes during prayers. Perhaps once eyes are shut, the most important cues to where they are and what they are doing are no longer visible and so the main way of connecting with the worship is lost. Some residents are not able to read the service but will lip-read. They can only do this if eye contact is maintained. Once you look away some may become lost and lose interest. For the leader this can be tricky if you are aware that there are several who need constant eye contact, but not all will want to respond at the same time. The answer is to be as sensitive as possible and 'tune in' to where they are.

The Christian Story

The readings I choose are familiar stories from the New Testament or passages from the Old Testament and offer assurance that despite everything God is still there and is constant in his love. The message should be positive: one of hope, love, peace and God's abiding presence. In our churches we most often centre on what our response should be to the love that God has shown us. When ministering to those with dementia it seems meaningful to celebrate God's great love for us and that he has made us the unique beings we are. That God remembers us, his children, means that we are important and of worth. This is particularly important for the confused. In the book of Isaiah God says, 'I will not forget you ... I have graven you on the palms of my hands' (Ch. 49:14–16). We worship a God who loves, understands and forgives.

Some argue that the Revised Authorised Version or the King James Version should be used. However, I have found that to be true only in very well-known passages like the 23rd Psalm. It is the way of reading that is important, drawing the listeners into the story and making it live. During one Good Friday service one lady began to comment on the words of the reading line by line, so I left spaces for her to do this. It was heartfelt on her part and very moving for me to be part of this experience.

Hymns are a very important part of the service. The music can trigger words from times long past and even in those who are unable to sing, a response can be seen. If you look carefully you may see a foot moving to the music, a nod of the head, or someone clapping. These are small signs that people are joining in and may bring a sense of comfort and reassurance to those who live in a world that has become increasingly alien to them. Hymns have to be chosen carefully. I had not thought of asking relatives if there were any special hymns that meant something to the resident until listening to them saying after a death, 'That was always his favourite hymn'. Why didn't I know, I wondered? But then I had not asked! Hymns with a strong tune, a repeated line or a chorus often work well, as do hymns that they would have known from school. 'All things bright and beautiful' and 'The Lord's my shepherd' are both favourites.

The hymn 'Tell me the old, old story' by Katherine Hankey (1834–1911), one that many in the Church have all but written off as Victorian sentimentality, can give us insight into the needs of those with dementia:

> Tell me the story simply, as to a little child; for I am weak and weary...
> Tell me the story slowly that I may take it in. Tell me the story often;
> for I forget so soon. Tell me the story always, if you would really be
> in any time of trouble a comforter to me. Tell me the old, old story, of
> Jesus and his love.

Relatives, visitors, staff and those from the Church need to be reminded of appropriate ways of retelling the Christian story in ways that will be understood.

There may be difficulties in providing music but this can be overcome by the use of hymns on tape. One such tape is distributed by Stirling Dementia Services at the University of Stirling, Scotland, and is called 'Loving Kindness in a Land of Forgetfulness'. It is a selection of well-known hymns produced for use in hospitals and homes for older people.

I usually include a talk in the service, of no more than five minutes and containing only one idea. I have found that taking objects in to illustrate a talk can bring surprising insights from residents. For example, the rotten fruit I took in for harvest led to 'Mr C' telling us about his compost heap where nothing is lost and decaying things go to make good soil. My theme was, 'Nothing is lost, and all in the end is harvest'.

The only aspect of worship I have not mentioned is Holy Communion. It was a step into the unknown when I was challenged to try it. I heard that one of the local clergy had decided not to offer communion to a resident as he believed the person no longer knew what it meant. I thought about what it was that we were offering in communion, the unconditional love of God in Jesus who died for us. I also considered at what other times we are reminded of this love of God for us, such as at the baptism of infants. We offer infant baptism as a sign of the love of God that is there for us before we can respond in any way: the prevenient love of God. Those with dementia are often prevented from responding to God's love, but in accepting the bread and wine they are receiving that prevenient love of God.

So, tentatively I began to think through how we would offer communion to those with dementia. The difficulties now appeared to be organisational and administrative. In talking it over with a colleague it was suggested that I use wafers and dip them into the wine during distribution. This I found wise as it made it easier for the resident to receive the bread and wine and the possibility of forgetting what was happening lessened. The printed service was too long so I decided to use an informal service based on the words Jesus used at the Last Supper as recorded in Paul's letter to the Corinthians.

Prayer:

LEADER: Loving God we give you thanks for your love to us. That
           even when we were far away you came to us in Jesus and
           welcomed us home. As we come to share the bread and the
           wine we pray that by the power of your Holy Spirit they
           may be for us the body and blood of Christ. Amen.

For we remember that on the night that Jesus was betrayed,
he took bread, gave you thanks, broke it and gave it to his
disciples saying, 'Take, eat. This is my body given for you;
do this in remembrance of me.' In the same way after supper
he took the cup and gave thanks and gave it to them saying,
'Drink this all of you. This is my blood of the new covenant
which is shed for you and for many for the forgiveness of
sins. Do this whenever you drink it, in remembrance of me'.
And so Lord, we do this in remembrance of him and
remember his death, until he comes again.

When we use the service I ask the Head of the Home to assist in the
distribution and we go to each person, who is then touched and asked by
name if they would like to receive the communion. Touching is so important,
as non-verbal communication is able to break through many barriers that
words simply reinforce. By naming the person I am affirming their identity
and that they are known and loved by God.

After all have received, I end with these words from the Methodist Service
Book: 'We thank you, Lord, that you have fed us in this sacrament, united us
with Christ, and given us a foretaste of the heavenly banquet prepared for all
people. Amen.'

When it came to the first Communion Service, despite all the preparation
I found that I still wondered what I was doing. Would they know what was
happening, especially if they were sitting behind me, or seemed to be asleep
for the whole service and had not seen the bread and wine? The words might
not make sense to them and they might in any case not know what the name
'Communion' means. My concerns proved to be unfounded. Some said 'yes'
and opened their mouths, others said 'no', and that was also good for a choice
had been made at a time in their lives when there are few areas in which
choices can be made. I made a point of asking one lady who delighted in
saying 'RC'. It reminded her of who she was and the tradition she belonged
to. Some became excited and some very grateful and asked God to bless me.

For me this was a very special experience. The level of response here was
in some ways more real than with a 'normal' congregation. This service takes
a little while, as time has to be given for each individual to respond to the
invitation to receive, but as yet I have had no one walk out or ask what is
going on. We share this service about once a month when I have planned to
be there. I have been told that the atmosphere in the Home is very different
after our service; there is a real sense of peace.

The service ends by saying the Grace together and then sharing the fellowship of the teapot! This is important as it enables us to mix socially and gradually take our leave. It has become a shared event. All have contributed in their own way and at the end of the afternoon we are all tired but affirmed in the love of God.

Worship for All?

Not all those who attended church before coming to Westbury want to be part of the service. One lady said, 'I've been to church for 50 years. I think that's enough!' She found it difficult to worship in a strange setting and it seemed to emphasise what in her life had been spoiled by dementia. Then there is 'Mrs M' who hovers in the background, wanting to be part of worship but not quite trusting herself to it. She had come to service the first few weeks she was at Westbury but at one service she had found the singing of a hymn too much and had cried. Now she keeps herself a little removed; her memories are too painful at the moment.

What we do at Westbury is to offer an opportunity for all who wish to worship God, to be reminded of the love that has been known and to be the people of God. However, the development of the service is not finished. We are still learning and changing the worship in the light of our experience.

Good Death

There are occasions when prayers are offered, or the communion shared with the resident and their family or friends, in their own room. This is especially the case when the resident is ill. Nuland in his book *How We Die* (1994, p.89f) suggests that the sadness seen in many with dementia is because they are mourning their own death. If we are to be of any use to such people then, faced with this deep sadness, we should not try to point them in a different direction that is more comfortable for us, but stay with them and feel their sadness. Prayers do not always need to be in words, but can be shared in silence.

On one visit I sat by 'Mrs A' who had recently had a stroke. She looked down at herself and then gave me a long hard look and said, 'Why?' At that moment there was no ambiguity in the question. I stopped, surprised by her clarity, then held the hand she offered me and said, 'I don't know'. We sat in silence until she released my hand, smiled and turned away.

When a resident is near to death there is often an almost constant vigil by staff and the relatives who are able to be there. We find that this is a special time, and as such is marked by prayers both in the Sunday Service and at the bedside.

> Dying is the most general human event, something we all have to do. But do we do it well? Is our death more than an unavoidable fate that we simply wished would not be there, or can it somehow become an act of fulfilment, perhaps more human than any other human act. (Nouwen 1994, p.14)

For the resident with dementia, death is often a gradual letting go: a becoming. There is no hurry. Time loses any meaning, but in the watching and waiting I have thought that it is like a birth, with the inner core of the person growing into death.

> Caring for the dying is saying: Don't be afraid, remember you are the Beloved Son of God. He will be there when you make your long jump ... Don't try to grab him, he will grab you ... just stretch out your arms and hands and trust, trust, trust. (Nouwen 1994, p.79)

When a resident dies, memories are often shared in their room with me by staff and prayers are said before the undertaker comes. We do this to give an ending to their time at Westbury and to help those staff who will be unable to come to the funeral. It is also important for friends in the Home to be able to pay their respects. I remember accompanying one lady whose friend had died; we went in together and repeated the Lord's Prayer.

Why Do We Bother?

In trying to find out as much as I could about dementia I came across a copy of *The Pastoral Care of the Mentally Ill* (Autton 1969, p.179) in which I looked up the term 'dementia' in the glossary of 'concepts and terms useful for priests'. The definition given was: 'generally used to refer to the advanced chronic cases of psychotic illness'. I went on to look up 'psychotic' and found that it was 'a severe mental disorder [in which] the sufferer has little or no insight into his condition'. I believe our appreciation of dementia has moved on since 1969 and much work has been done on the implications of this for care of the individual.

From the outside it appears that those with dementia are totally dependent upon others and unable to give anything to a relationship. Despite this, those who are able to give time to be with the person with dementia often find that they have received so much more than they have given. The 'spiritual' refers to whatever is the very essence of each human being, and Ellor (1997) writes that 'Spiritual well-being is the affirmation of life in a relationship with God, self, community, and environment that nurtures and celebrates wholeness' (p.2). So good spiritual care has to tap into the feelings and memories.

Spirituality is also about our relationship with the Divine. For most people the Divine is 'out there' but to the person with dementia it is most certainly 'within' them. Their world-view becomes narrowed, some would say self-centred. Spirituality can be found in a service of worship, which may or may not bring back memories. The real benefit, and the greatest gift we can offer in the services is to help them find their true spirituality, that of God within them, a God who remembers, knows and loves them. Autton (1969) quotes a remark made by Evelyn Underhill that:

> Many a congregation, when it assembles for worship ... must look to the angels like a muddy, puddley shore at low tide; littered with every kind of rubbish and odds and ends – a distressing sort of spectacle. And then the tide of worship comes in, and it's all gone; the dead sea-urchins and jelly fish, the paper and the empty cans and the nameless bits of rubbish. The cleansing sea flows over the whole lot. (p.131)

Continuing Evaluation

The service has now been used for three years so I have begun to look at the service more critically in the light of experience. This is not easy as there are so many variables to any observed response, especially that of measuring recognition. It would depend on what relationship there was with the person leading worship; how they felt on that afternoon; if the chosen hymns or readings were familiar; and almost more important than any of the others, if they were sitting next to someone who could help them to be involved in worship.

It was found that the response by those with dementia to our worship was greatly aided by contact with another, usually a member of staff or a visitor who could draw him/her into the service. Results from Weldon and Bellinger (1997) on collaborative and individual processes of remembering show that recall is significantly higher in groups than as an individual and that when remembering takes place as a social activity this also guides the process and the content of retrieval. This supports our decision at Westbury to offer an act of collective worship which others suggested was a waste of time as those with dementia were not able to respond. Someone else coming in to do this evaluation would possibly have different findings since, having knowledge of the residents, I was able to link certain actions/movements to other times when I had observed them recognise someone/something. This is in some ways a disadvantage as it makes drawing a scientific conclusion almost impossible. However, what was shown was that, although conventional care would seem to suggest that someone with dementia would not be able to respond to new forms of worship, in the case of those at Westbury they had in some way learned the service and were able to use their automatic memory as well as recall in order to respond.

Research has been done by Nelson, Bennett and Xu (1997) into recollective and automatic uses of memory and they have found that the recollective uses of memory benefit from full as opposed to divided attention. They also found that the use of cues was an important factor in enabling recall.

Other research has shown that the leading of worship has to be very clear and direct, and as simple and straightforward as possible, so as not to cause confusion. It has been found that dementia patients with Alzheimer's-type dementia were distracted by a varied visual display. It appeared that 'they simply could not cope with the extra processing involved, and suffered an "information overload"' (Stuart-Hamilton 1994, p.156).

It is important that evaluation continues to take place as there are still questions that need to be addressed. For example, some residents at Westbury are very disabled by the effects of dementia. Some are unable to speak or move independently, so is there any advantage to their well-being to be gained from disturbing them from their normal routine and bringing them to the service? I find such questions disturbing since it is so much easier for those who care for them to leave them where they are if they are content. But if they are able to be at the service and 'soak up' the atmosphere, perhaps this would enhance their spiritual well-being.

I feel that we learn every time a new resident comes to us. Each is a unique individual with likes and dislikes that are respected. Instinctively, I feel that the answer to the question I posed is that it all depends! It all depends on the individual and on the care staff being 'in tune' with their needs. Those with dementia are not empty vessels but people with their own history, present and future, and should not be categorised by the dementia they have.

The vision we have for our service at Westbury is that we seek to reach out to those who are in need and, with the help of God's Spirit, to heal what is broken and reunite what is separate, enabling them to gain strength from the community to which they belong.

'O give thanks to the Lord for he is good: his mercy endures for ever.'
Psalm 107:1

CHAPTER 12

Memory, Personhood and Faith

Paul H. Wilson

The door opened and I was greeted by Alan and Barbara. Alan took me through the kitchen and stopped at his wife's activity table. On it were simple jigsaws, crayons, paper and materials. Alan told me how Barbara (the names are pseudonyms) spent an hour or so at a time at the table. He celebrated all she could do. As we spoke, a video of Pavarotti was playing in the lounge. We stood and watched as Barbara joyfully danced, totally unaware of or uninhibited by our presence. Alan spoke of her love of music and the enjoyment she received from the video, dancing and singing along to it. He expressed the hope that one day she would play the piano again. We sat down in the lounge and Barbara, the homemaker, went around all the pictures in the room, telling me about each one in great detail, but unfortunately, her speech was jumbled. Barbara is suffering from dementia.

Alan spoke fondly about his wife, celebrating her gifts and abilities, sharing the pain and difficulties of their life but playing them down.

After sharing an hour together, I offered to pray. Barbara knelt down in front of me and took my hands in hers. We prayed together. Afterwards she gave me a hug and in the clearest speech thanked me for praying for her. Alan informed me that every night they prayed together, for prayer meant so much. Alan and Barbara try to come to our early morning communion service where people will understand their situation.

Seven years of ministering to those with dementia and their families has provided insights into 'Memory, Personhood and Faith'. Reflecting upon the impact of dementia on a person enables us to reflect upon our own humanity and faith.

Barbara offers us the opportunity to see that dementia can be like the autumn. As you walk down a country lane, the leaves are falling but if you look closely buds are present, waiting to burst into new life. Even though the leaves are lost, the recognisable structure of a particular tree remains.

Dementia causes many faculties to fail like the leaves falling from the tree, but buds remain and the structure, the essential core of their being, is often recognisable. Person-centred care encourages caregivers to look for the buds and the structures within a person, celebrating abilities rather than emphasising disabilities. The ethos of such care is to act as their 'memory', creating an environment which they would have known as familiar and seeking to ensure that the values upon which they based their life are respected. In so doing, people are placed in a positive environment, one in which they do not continually fail and one which is familiar to them.

Dementia is not a continuum of ageing. It is a pathological disease of the brain. It does, however, bear some changes (though often accelerated into a short time span) shared with the ageing process. The autumn of life is a time of great change. It is marked by loss of family and friends, perhaps loss of self-worth and purpose in retirement, illness and the ageing process. Ageing may create a loss of independence and greater dependence upon others. Yet ageing is not and should not be regarded as a negative experience. Many experience good health well into their eighties and nineties, with new opportunities for interests, travel and time for relationships with families. Yet the effects of change, loss and suffering loss are some of the issues, amongst many, which people need to face and reflect upon, perhaps with the aid of family, a friend or caring professional.

The loss of memory is an existential fear for most people. The able-bodied feel that they could cope with disability but not the loss of memory. They are expressing that within the body is that which is essentially the 'I'. This 'I' has interacted with the environment and people, learning continually from those experiences. When memory is lost, 'I' loses contact not only with the environment and people but the 'I' itself. 'I' is unable to generate itself the cues to release the memories or to schedule them in chronological time. The person with dementia is within a never-ending learning experience which may result in exhaustion and withdrawal. Memory is a key component within the understanding of 'I'.

Person-centred care, as proposed by Tom Kitwood and the Bradford Dementia Centre, has created an ethos where, in simplistic terms, the caregiver provides the environment in which the person has dignity, is free to be to the best of their ability and is treated within an 'I–Thou' relationship. The dementia sufferer is a person and not a problem, to be cared for and not managed. The environment created is based on cues which place the person in touch with the 'I' within them. Through reminiscence and validation, the person is placed in contact with 'the basic core characteristics that made them the person they always were' (Bell and McGregor 1995). Communication is encouraged and validated and a relationship encouraged between the caregiver and person with dementia. Alan, without reading the books, is caring for the person who could be hidden within the problems they face together. He seeks to place Barbara within an environment in which she is kept in touch with the 'I' within her. Music, art, prayer and love are but elements of that which is 'I' for her.

Person-centred care is not restricted to those with dementia. It is an ethos of care which should be available to everyone. In the Judaeo-Christian tradition, a person is the interaction between body, mind and spirit. Factors affecting any one of these aspects, which are interrelated, can create dis-ease within the person. To maintain a sense of wholeness the needs of the body, mind and spirit must be taken into account. The concept of wholeness, should not be restricted to a state of perfection. A move towards wholeness can be achieved whilst living within limitations. The Jewish term 'shalom', translated, 'peace', is a word which describes wholeness. Denis Duncan describes it as 'the totality of our relationship – to God "upwards", to the earth "downwards", to others "outwards" and to ourselves "inwards"' (Duncan 1988). Shalom is the blessing of all the relationships in which we live. The aim of care could therefore be to promote shalom in a person.

Care-giving is thus more than the provision of a safe environment and communication with others; it is also the provision of spiritual care to nurture the person in the journey within and pastoral care to nurture the person in the journey above. Spiritual care and pastoral care may or may not share the same ideals and goals.

Dementia care works on the principle of the person following the same patterns of growth as those ageing without the loss of memory. It shares the principle of enabling a person to process the spiritual tasks of old age. A major task is to face unresolved problems from the past. This falls within Erikson's eighth and final stage of his theory of the development of persons. He calls this 'Ego Integrity v. Despair' (Erikson 1963). As a person engages in life review there will be episodes which they wish had never happened or had turned out in a different way. People express this in a desire to turn the clock back. Regrettably we cannot. What has happened has happened and the consequences may continue to affect the person in an adverse way. In the final stage of life, such life events are faced again.

Rather than continuing to express despair over what happened, Erikson's aim is that the person accepts that the life event was enacted at a certain time, based on information and emotions which were time orientated. If the event happened again the consequences would be different because the person involved has developed. If a person on reflection accepts the historical nature of the event and their human fallibility at that particular moment, the person can be released from the continuing effect of despair and set free to face the future without a sense of fear. The effects of the life event may be resolved within them. Within this stage the person comes to accept the events of their life as something that had to be. The experience of wishing we could turn the clock back is common to all, even though we know that we cannot do so. Instead we need to accept the events and be freed from their effect in our life's journey. For Erikson, the person needs to express comradeship with those events as events of the past which were products of those times.

Reflective reminiscence in the ageing process is part of coming to terms with the events of life. People seek to develop an understanding of the meaning of their life and resolve issues. Each person is in the process of letting go and coming to terms with their past and their present.

Spiritual care involves a willingness to accompany a person on this inward reflective journey. The person is exploring the ground and purpose of their being. This need not, however, bear any reference to God. For a person may have lived their life without acknowledging the concept of God as the ground of their being. Spiritual tasks still need to be undertaken. The accompanist listens, reflects, validates and enables the person to resolve as best they can the memories which have arisen.

Spiritual care also involves the identification of values on which a person has based their life. Sean Buckland offers the metaphor of the 'fragile web of well-being' (Buckland 1995). The metaphor was offered in the context of dementia care but again gives insight into the spiritual care of all who are ageing. The web of well-being is made up of strands of strength and positive experience. These are the resources developed since birth which are the very core of our being. New experiences or resolution of damaging experiences result in new strands of the web. These grow in strength as a person gains confidence and a sense of value. If the web is strong enough it will succeed in containing damage and pain. Some damaging experiences will break through and will remain as unresolved experiences.

A living environment needs to take into account the effects that change and the ageing process are having upon the person. Agitation or anger with a situation or withdrawal are signs of ill-being. The person should be enabled to explore the values and practices which have helped the person to cope with life in the past. Reflection on life history can enable the person to come to terms with change, bereavement, growing dependency or disability. The strands of the web enable the accompanist or caregiver to understand personality, likes and dislikes, belief and practices and key events which are milestones in the development of the person.

For those with dementia or communication problems, this information may be collated from family and friends rather than reflective listening. By building a person's values into care-giving, the person is not placed into an environment which is foreign to their lifestyle.

Baltes' theory of life development (Baltes and Reese 1982) offers three areas which affect the development of a person. Normative age-graded development is the basic development one would expect in any individual in terms of biological ageing. Normative historical-graded experience includes those events which had a particular effect upon a generation, for example the Second World War. The third area is non-normative life development, the effects of major events in a person's life which are unique to that individual. Whilst the first two factors may be known, the third needs to be pieced together. This can be gained by attending to a person's life story. For those with dementia, family and friends are key resources.

Spiritual care involves listening and reflecting upon the life's events, seeking to resolve unresolved episodes in a person's life and the questions of suffering, loss and preparation for death. This is care which must be available to all. It is neither a need confined to the religious nor a type of care provided by the religious. Such care is often provided by family, friends, the caring professions and religious communities. Berggren-Thomas and Griggs state, 'Spiritual care is part of the basic holistic care nurses provide for all clients. Whether it is through attentive listening, prayer for or with them or mere conversation, nurses allow their spirits to touch those of the clients and assist them along the path of spiritual growth' (Berggren-Thomas and Griggs 1995).

This calls for an 'I–Thou' relationship, where two persons are interacting and both the 'I' and the 'Thou' are affected and possibly changed by the interaction. This requires openness, trust and vulnerability in both the person remembering and reflecting and the one listening and attending. Some would not wish, or do not have the skills, to enter into such a relationship, but express their love and care perhaps in other practical ways. People with different gifts are required in the totality of caring for the person; each is important and it would be wrong to grade these gifts in any way.

Pastoral care has an added dimension. It is not set over and against other forms of care. It is distinctive in function rather than in a qualitative way. That function is to assure the person of the love of God in their present situation. Alistair Campbell defines the aim of pastoral care as, 'To help people to know love, both as something to be received and as something to give' (Campbell 1985). The context in which this love is revealed is in sacrament, prayer and prophecy. In pastoral care God is declared as present, in prayer He is the one able to transform life, and in justice equality of persons is sought for all.

Whilst evangelistic zeal might urge us to declare God present to all, that may only be appropriate for the vast majority in the living witness of being present in practical care and listening ears. In order to gain respect and validity within the totality of care, sensitivity to our partners and colleagues is important. At a stage when doors are being opened to person-centred care, respect must be developed by secular organisations for the gifts the Church can offer. For those whose lives have been centred upon and transformed by faith in God, there is a responsibility to proclaim the love of God in word and sacrament. This added dimension is expected by those of the faith community, acknowledged by secular organisations and may gradually be requested as relationships develop with others. It should not, however, be imposed. Pastoral care takes the sermon to the individual, declaring not only the universality of God's love but the particularity of that love for the individual.

Faith for many is a major component of the 'I'. During life's journey, faith has helped strengthen the web of well-being. The metaphor of the cairn is helpful in this area. On mountains, cairns are often found. They provide comfort to later travellers, that the way has been travelled before and safety found at this point. Travellers add their stones to the cairn. The 'I' may have particular moments in their lives which, if returned to, provide assurance that the way has been travelled before and is safe. The stones of the cairn may be a hymn, bible reading, place or photograph which, when returned to, gives hope for the future. Travellers of all ages need to be offered the opportunity to tell their stories and gain strength from the memory of those moments which have been a revelation of God's love for them.

The pastoral care of the ageing is as important a ministry within the Church as any other. The pastoral visit, not just confined to clergy, is essential for listening to the spiritual needs. As memories are revisited and explored, the pastoral visit not only reflects upon the information given but also the insights into the nature of God. People and events can be reflected upon and prayed for. The offer of confession, forgiveness and absolution can release the person to live free from the guilt which may have enslaved them for many years.

In the development of the 'I' of the person of faith, using the example of Baltes' development theory, there are three elements. There is the general theme of the revelation of God in scripture and creation. There may be historical strands which have affected a generation (e.g. The Billy Graham Crusade, Iona). There are also individual experiences of God. Each have affected and been part of the development of 'I'.

Pastoral care takes into account these influences and seeks to enable the person to encounter God in the questions they are asking. The pastoral caregiver is not seeking to impose answers but to present God. The book of Job teaches everyone not to judge but to seek to reveal God and His love to the person.

Christian faith is upheld by reminding someone continually of the story of God's relationship with humanity. Adoration, confession, supplication, petition and intercession, indeed every component of worship, is a response to the revealed nature of God declared again in scripture and sacrament. By telling the story, we keep before the people the memory of God's dealings with humanity. Charles Elliott describes the Church as 'the ark in which the memory of God's dealing with his people is stored'. He continues that the other functions are to tell the story, live the story and interpret the story to each and every generation (Elliott 1995). He argues that the memory of God, when brought alongside the memory of nations and individuals, tempers, critiques and changes the memory. In this way, memory is atoned and salvation is realised. Salvation and wholeness are one and the same.

Memories are not perfect accounts of events. They are selective interpretations, tainted and disabled by our sinfulness, centring the events upon our self. They are remembered in a biased way. The occasions a person hurts us far outweigh the good they have done for us for they are dwelt upon, blown out of all proportion. Hurts unwittingly inflicted may be carried around for life, colouring our perceptions of people and their actions. Memories, therefore, need to be critiqued, challenged and cleansed by the memory of Christ. Our mindset needs to be renewed by the continual challenge of Christ's teaching, His example and His self-sacrifice. Exposure to these through worship, fellowship and personal devotions is used by the

Holy Spirit to remind us of what Christ said and did and by an act of the will, discipline and submission to that example and rule, actions and patterns can be transformed. This is an example of Paul's renewal of the mind.

In pastoral care, the memories of an individual are challenged by the memory of God. Events which are remembered and revisited can be reinterpreted under the memory of God and release and forgiveness found.

A lady in her eighties was diagnosed as having lung cancer with only days to live. I immediately provided home communion. The passage selected was Isaiah 43:1–7. After communion, as her daughter made a drink of tea, she thanked me for the reading. She spoke of death, her suffering and the intense pain. Her faith remained that through it all God would be with her. She highlighted the phrases, 'You are precious in my sight, and because I love you … do not be afraid for I am with you'. She clung to that in the darkest moments. The content of the communal memory was retold and helped her through the last days of her life.

Worship through specialised techniques of knowing personal faith history and using all the senses through taste (Eucharist), sight (symbols), hearing (music and word), smell (scents), touch (soothing contact) can remind a person of God.

Arthur and Jean were celebrating their fifty-third wedding anniversary. Arthur, suffering from dementia, was unaware of the day. As I visited them, Jean told me of the day and I asked what their wedding hymn had been. We had found over a couple of years that hymns had been the gateway for Arthur to express faith and enter into prayer and communion. I sang the first line and Arthur joined in singing the tenor line word and note perfect. After he finished, he leaned across and gave Jean a kiss and said, 'I love you'. We prayed, thanking God for their marriage and we all shared in the Lord's Prayer. I left them both enjoying the moment. Jean asked for this story to be told wherever it may help people to realise that even in severe dementia the 'I' can be reached and love and faith expressed.

Memory enables us to access the events, people, emotions and faith which with other unconscious building blocks make the 'I', the individual person. All that is experienced affects our personhood. Memory needs to be accessed, nurtured and remembered. Family, community and national stories need to be told and retold to maintain our identity. The telling of personal stories is not only important but may be therapeutic, if not now then later, in accompanying someone in the latter stages of their life's journey.

Reminiscing is a feature of ageing, not in terms of merely living in the past, although this may be less painful than the present, but also in making sense of our lives. The retracing of the steps on life's journey is a spiritual experience, exposing the relationship with oneself. Care must include the accompaniment and reflective listening. Pastoral care includes the interaction of the memory of God, the representation of God and his activity to offer hope, love and His presence on the journey.

The Church in its ongoing ministry must value the personhood of each of her members. Through the ministry of the whole people, the ageing must be accompanied on their journey. Whilst others may care for their physical and environmental well-being, the Church may contribute to the relationship with themselves and must contribute to their relationship with God. In the same way that specialist ministries for the young and various chaplaincies are developed, so specialist insights for accompanying the ageing must form part of the training of clergy and lay pastoral visitors alike. The aim of care for the ageing should be wholeness, including mind and spirit, areas of memory and faith. Within the totality of care, the Church continues to have a distinctive and important role which it must claim and fulfil, releasing resources to minister to the whole person in the autumn of their life.

CHAPTER 13

Joy in the Moment

Immediacy and Ultimacy in Dementia

C. Mary Austin

Introduction

It was Freda's birthday – we all gathered together for the weekly service of Holy Communion in the EMI unit of the geriatric hospital of which I am the Free Church Chaplain. How old was she? She couldn't remember – perhaps she was 84. 'It was 89 when we asked you earlier,' joked someone. It didn't matter – we sang 'Happy Birthday' and continued with the service. A short while later I read the 23rd Psalm; Freda joined in, reciting from memory, word for word!

Joy in the Moment

Alzheimer's disease and other forms of dementia rob their victims of their cognitive reasoning powers; gradually the dementing person loses insight into their condition and doesn't even remember that they have forgotten. The ability to verbalise feelings is lost but, as far as we know and from observation of sufferers as well as listening to those in earlier stages of the disease, the ability to feel remains acute – pain and sorrow, joy and laughter are part of living for the dementing as well as the rest of us. Memories from the past come bubbling up in disjointed fragments and the sufferer is on a journey to a point where, in the severe stages of the disease, past, present and future coalesce into an eternal 'now'.

If 'now' is a bad experience, that is the whole of life; it is therefore for those responsible for the welfare of the dementing to see that 'now' is good, to provide the necessary prompts to give good feelings – to enable a sense of 'Joy in the Moment'. Obviously a major part of this for the carer is to provide for physical well-being, a loving, caring environment where the sufferer's physical needs for shelter, food, warmth and security are catered for. But life is more than clothing – and even into the furthest depths of dementia the sufferer has spiritual needs also. We all have spiritual needs – the need to be loved and to love, to forgive and be forgiven, to find purpose in life – whether or not we choose to express them in some form of religion. For today's dementia sufferer, formal religion is likely to have a place in their spiritual experience even if only through school assembly or Sunday School. This may well have given them a sense of the presence of God which has sustained them through the ups and downs of life.

Many such a person can be enabled to know a sense of the presence of God, to find 'Joy in the Moment' through simple acts of worship: the sound of familiar hymn tunes, as for Freda, the words of the 23rd Psalm or the Lord's Prayer; the sights and tastes and smells associated with worship – candles, the cross, incense, a rosary and, most of all, bread and wine. For those of other faith the prompts will be different but no less important. For such worship to mediate something of the love of God, the value of the individual and above all, a sense of peace is to bring 'Joy in the Moment'. As with Freda, many sufferers can, with help, sustain their spiritual life throughout the illness. For many, even those not regular churchgoers, we have found a weekly service of Holy Communion both appreciated and beneficial, and many have 'come back' to church through it.

In the light of a faith, in which hope for the future depends on memory of the past, such 'Joy in the Moment' speaks of the sacrament of the present moment and gives a glimpse of the timelessness of eternity. It is life lived in the present – or the distant past – but in a lack of awareness of the passing of time; so different from our lives which, so obsessed with the past and the future, frequently miss the present moment and the presence of God in it. Our pace of life precludes 'stopping and staring' which is all the demented person may do all day. Perhaps we can learn from them and be slowed in our frenetic race to the future as we repeatedly reflect on the past.

The care of the demented, whilst arduous and difficult, does repay in such ways. Alison Froggatt (Froggatt and Shamy 1992) reflects that 'wherever there are signs of loving relationships, however limited, surely these can be seen as signs of God's love at work; if we stop to acknowledge this we affirm the reality of the Kingdom of Heaven here'. And she quotes the words of a carer: 'I believe the time I spent looking after my mother was perhaps the most valuable experience of my life. It has given me a glimpse of a shadow of another reality, something outside the material world. Something that cannot be perceived by any of the five senses, yet can make itself known to our innermost self.'

Except You Be Like Little Children

Shakespeare in *As You Like It* suggests that the final state of life 'is second childishness and mere oblivion: sans teeth, sans eyes, sans taste, sans everything'.

This is an understandable reaction to the demented person who is unable to do anything for themselves and has little or no speech or understanding. Yet it is to demean the sufferer to think in terms of second childhood and it is a wrong approach to treat sufferers like children. They are mature adults with a lifetime of experience. However, there are insights to be gained in reflecting on Jesus' attitude to and words about children. Perhaps the sufferer in their apparent second childhood is closer to the Kingdom of Heaven than we. Jesus said that we must be childlike.

We may feel concern about the faith of a person no longer able to sustain an awareness of the presence of God or even to know that God exists. Our faith is one of a relationship which is said to require response. However, we don't have the same concerns about babies but baptise them as a sign of the prevenient grace of God. In the same way the dementia sufferer with no sense of self is still a valued child of God.

'Are your wonders known in the darkness or your saving help in the land of forgetfulness?' (Psalm 88) wonders the Psalmist. God assures us in the words of Isaiah:

> I have called you by name ... you are precious in my sight. (43:1,4)

> Can a woman forget her nursing child, or show no compassion for the child of her womb? Even these may forget, yet I will not forget you. See I have inscribed you on the palms of my hands. (49:15f)

Assurance indeed that God remembers your name when you cannot even remember it yourself!

And then the End

Our Christian faith is one of hope, ultimately the hope of a life after death secure in the love of God. Everything tradition and scripture teaches is that we will experience this life, that it will be subjective. What then for the demented, who have no sense of self before death? Will they know themselves? If we believe with Pailin (1986) that life after death is merely objective, that we live on for ever in the memory of God, there is no problem. However, the question arises as to whether we have any sense ourselves of continuing existence. Pailin suggests that if there is to be subjective immortality as the continuing being of the person, it would seem to have to be the continuation of the ongoing and cumulative tradition of remembered and forgotten experiences, responses and decisions that must occur. So what happens when there is no memory?

For centuries the western world has taken for its model of personhood the Platonic philosophy of the immortal soul which is residing for a while within a physical body. Such dualism has led to all sorts of violations of the body, suppression of its appetites and a general devaluing of creation as merely a training ground for the soul's continual life in heaven, preparation for which is the sole purpose of life. However, scripture speaks of wholeness and, in line with modern anthropological thinking, of the whole person, of a single unity or being. This has profound implications for the dementia sufferer.

First, the concept of a soul or mind inhabiting a body can be very reassuring when the physical body starts to fail, but very frightening when it is the mind which starts to fail, as though the very sense of being is lost. Biblical theology of the whole person helps our understanding of the personhood of the dementia sufferer. The Church of England Board of Social Responsibility in its report, *Ageing* (1990), addresses personhood in confusion with the statement that the Church must 'provide theoretical understanding of the nature of humanity which does not rely on our rationality though this must be a part of it', and suggests that symbolic interpretation may help change attitudes such as the kingdom being open to children.

One such model is that of the scapegoat where the dementia sufferer carries the responsibility for the breakdown of relationships and in whom, if we care to look, we can all see a reflection of ourselves. Our fear of dementia is in seeing within it a mirror of our own brokenness. When we dare to look we see reflected our own powerlessness, fear, need of love, our hopelessness and despair. We should not fear seeing ourselves reflected in the demented but use the experience better to know ourselves, to recognise the echoes of needs deep within ourselves, which is necessary if we are not to be shut off to those needs in others – something which enables growth in the carer.

Personhood for the dementia sufferer is no less than for the rest of us 'in the image of God'. Vanstone's theology (1982) offers in Christ's passion and death a model of a God-in-waiting, a passive God in whose image are the sick and dying and broken.

Second, if we understand the human person as a whole being, in line with the biblical model and supported by modern thinking, as opposed to the Platonic philosophy of an immortal soul, we must believe that at death the whole person, the whole being, dies. Death is a serious event. Yet it is an entirely natural one: death and decay are part of creation, not the result of its fall. They are the means by which life continues and develops. Without death there can be no new life, without death there would be no evolution. John Bowker (1991) suggests that if we contemplate our hand, there are in it atoms that came from a distant star in the universe billions of years ago. Without the death of that star we would not exist. It is all part of the cycle of life.

It is not as Glenn Weaver (1986) suggests, that the decline of dementia is a return to the chaos which preceded creation. He maintains that 'slow physical deterioration and loosened social relationships have profound spiritual significance, for they can separate a person from God'. A person can certainly feel separated from God but, although progression of the disease might seem like a descent into chaos, this cannot be in the theological sense as opposed to creation. We want to confirm the continued wholeness in the brokenness of the confused person. Such is no more a descent into chaos than the disease and subsequent degeneration of any organ of the body leading eventually to death.

Death, therefore, is natural and final, but Christians believe that what God has created once, God can recreate, that new life can be raised, not in a crude reanimation of flesh and bone but in a sense that we cannot understand, with which St Paul struggles in his writing about spiritual bodies (1 Cor. 15), but in which we can have confidence and hope. Althaus, quoted by Kung (1982), speaks of the 'indissolubility of the personal relationship with God' which is not a question of 'the soul' but of the person as a living unit of corporeal-mental being founded by God's 'call'.

Howatch (1997) in her novel *A Question of Integrity* puts this concept into more user-friendly language. When we speak of body in terms of life after death we are using the term as a code word for the whole person: 'When we say "anybody" or "everybody" or "somebody" we're not just talking about flesh and blood – we're referring to the complex pattern of information which the medium of flesh and blood expresses.'

The experience of many caring for people with dementia offers tangible although anecdotal evidence for resurrection. Carers have spoken of a lifting of dementia close to death. I was told of a man without language who in the last moments of his life spoke the words of the 23rd Psalm. Eileen Shamy's mother at the end, clear eyed, said firmly 'God never forgets us; remember that, dear' (Froggatt and Shamy, 1992). A friend speaks of her mother who gently and rationally said 'goodbye' to her. I have also experienced and heard stories of others who in death seem in some way to be healed, though obviously from the pathological point of view evidence of disease would still be present. We often speak of death as the ultimate healing – perhaps it is as if we see a glimpse of that healing, a glimpse of resurrection in the moment of death.

If the whole of the person with dementia has died, God can resurrect that which is truly the being of that person, and life after death is not dependent on a continuing of mind or understanding or self-awareness. The processes of dementia are physical degeneration of the brain which affects the mind. However, modern science sees the totality of the being and mind as more than the physical processes. Bowker (1991) and Harpur (1991) both describe this in writing on death and life after death. Bowker says that, although memory is a strong candidate for the self-perceived persistence of identity, it is not in fact a sufficient or even necessary condition for the human sense of being one's self. He doesn't refer to dementia but does allow that people can lose their memory and still have a sense of self. He shows how Oliver Sacks (1982) in his book *Awakenings*, about the experience of victims of encephalitis lethargica who had been in a condition of zombie-like passivity for up to 50 years until they were awakened by the drug L-DOPA, describes the awakening as something happening to a person and not simply the dormant machinery in the head.

Bowker rejects the concept of the immortal soul but suggests that in the understanding of the whole person described above there is a relationship of mind to brain which enables a person to be the agent of their own activity and subject of their own experience. This, he says, continues through the process of death in the experience of those pronounced clinically dead and then resuscitated. Even in life the cells of our bodies are continually being renewed yet our continuation as one being is affirmed from experience.

The concept of resurrection is a difficult one. St Paul struggled with it, as have countless theologians, and so we do not claim to make it any clearer! Howatch offers two useful models from the modern world. From the sphere of computers her character speaks of flesh and blood as becoming superfluous after death and the pattern of the whole as being downloaded elsewhere. A further illustration speaks of great art: 'think of Michelangelo ... In the Sistine Chapel he expressed a vision by creating, through the medium of paint, patterns of colour. The paint is of vital importance but in the end it's the pattern that matters and the pattern which can be reproduced in another medium such as a book or film.'

Harpur affirms a sense of new life and being, a spiritual body which holds some continuum with earthly life. A long discussion of the secular and different religious evidences and beliefs concerning life after death brings him back to the claims of scripture that our hope lies in the resurrection of Christ, and that we too, with the whole of humanity, will rise. This is no blind acceptance based on a view of the authority of scripture but one deemed reasonable in the face of experience and belief and the search for evidence for life after death.

However, he concedes that from a scientific point of view there is no proof. For Harpur, it is because of his deep faith in the 'reality Whom we call God' and in the kind of God revealed by the teachings of Judaism, Christianity and Islam that he is 'persuaded of the truth of spiritual places beneath, through, and beyond this world of space, sense and time'. For this reason he believes:

> God has a destiny for each of us that transcends the grave ... in a dimension of being where all of life's promises will be fulfilled, not because of our inner merit or innate immortality, but because of God's faithfulness and love. Because God is God, the forces of evil, disease, decay and death do not have the last word. (Harpur 1991, p.260)

This is based on an understanding that in the historical story of the suffering, death and resurrection of Jesus we find the mythical statement of the deepest truths about the spiritual journey of each one of us. When St Paul says that he no longer lives but 'Christ lives in me', he is referring to his identification with the principle of dying to a materialistic or physical existence and rising to a life lived according to the values and call of the Spirit. Harpur points out the relevance of this to daily living as well as to a final destiny. It is a case of us being absorbed into the dying and rising of Christ, that Christ is in us and in a very real sense there is a moving towards divinity for us all. In the resurrection of Christ we see a model of our own resurrection, with Christ as the first fruits, as St Paul puts it.

What a life after death will be like is left to the fiction writers and those who purport to write fact but whose writings are too bizarre to be taken seriously. We simply trust, again in Harpur's words, that 'we will return to the source of our being not as rivers return to the ocean and are swallowed by it, but as recognisable individuals', a notion expressed by Eliot (1963) in his poem 'Little Gidding' as a journey of exploration, the end of which is to arrive at the beginning yet know it as never before.

Harpur concludes that 'the deepest longings of all our hearts will be satisfied. Meanwhile, we can safely entrust ourselves, our loved ones, and all the human community to the grace and mercy of God'. 'No eye has seen nor ear heard, nor the human heart conceived what God has prepared for those who love him' (1 Cor. 2:9). We are speaking of nothing less than new creation, the transformation of the whole person by God's life creating Spirit. In Harpur's words, not 'a release from corporeality but released with and in a now glorified spiritualised corporeality – a new creation'.

This affirms hope for new life for us all, demented as well as those who die from other causes, which is grounded in belief in the resurrection of Jesus. The belief that the Christ, whose passion and suffering on the cross enables Him to identify with the demented, was also raised to life, offers them and their carers the hope of the transformation of good through and out of suffering and new life in and through their death.

And so to Care

Dementia challenges our deepest perceptions of personhood. Carers look on helpless as the beloved slips away, changing personality, eventually not even recognising those who love them. It challenges our faith in God, and as with all suffering we grope to find God in it. We also struggle to find purpose in such a cruel disease and are rendered powerless by our own inability to help. Visits seem futile when they are quickly forgotten, conversation impossible. Yet in our caring we can help provide that 'Joy in the Moment' for the sufferer; our care for them is a service to the dying, much the same as when a woman poured expensive perfume on Jesus' head. The world perceived it as waste!

And so two poems I have written: the first in the context of the tragic death of a teenager, the second in the form of a creed.

I Don't Understand

This Life
This Death
This fragile humanity
So very alive
Suddenly no more
What meaning in life
Where is God?
Young life so cruelly extinguished
Old life vacuous
Unknowing
And unknown
What were you years ago?
You who sit and gesture
Torment on your face
You grasp my hand
and I am helpless
In the face of your anguish
Where is God?
Where is God in your confused mind
Your inability to communicate.
You pluck obsessively at your skirt
Revealing stocking tops
Undignified
Skirts that once children tugged
Legs that once danced and ran
Where is your life?
Where is God?
Young life extinguished
Old life lingering?
Is your life meaningless?
Do you know pleasure?
I only see torment in your toothless face.
So where is God?
I don't understand
I only know that he is here
With the depth of my being
I know he cares and

Suffers too
That Christ is in you
Nailed to a cross
But I don't understand.

What a waste!?

We believe in the God who created and sustains the universe
Who holds it in his loving care
For whom each is his beloved child
Valued
Whoever they are
Wherever they are
Whether they know it or not.
And so we believe in the God who loves
Who loves those society fears
Who loves those who are different
In all their broken humanity
And powerlessness
We see this in the revelation of Christ
In whom God was reconciling the world.
And so it is not a waste to care
Not a waste to love
Not a waste to give time to the needs
Of one who is confused
To bring them indeed
A presence of Christ
To 'anoint them with oil'
And bring ...
Joy in the Moment ...
In the Land of Forgetfulness.

CHAPTER 14

Dementia

A Challenge to Christian Theology
and Pastoral Care

Malcolm Goldsmith

The Relevance of Theology

I cut my theological teeth in the 1960s, which was a wonderful time to begin
one's ordained ministry. There was hope in the air, there was an atmosphere
of theological excitement and expectancy, old ideas were being challenged
and new ideas were coming to the fore within a context of reassessing the
meaning of mission. Bonhoeffer (1953) was being read and reread, a martyr
within our own lifetime. Harvey Cox's (1965) *The Secular City* was
challenging us to look at our society with new eyes, and the World Council
of Churches dictum of 'Let the World Provide the Agenda' was being either
enthusiastically espoused or energetically challenged. 'Honest to God' was
encouraging theology to be taken seriously by 'ordinary people' and 'South
Bank Religion' was providing an antidote to the sense that the Church was as
it always had been and would remain so forever! We were living in a world
dominated by the Vietnam War, Martin Luther King was marching, there was
an obvious relevance for the Gospel in a world being shaped and moulded by
oppressive forces. And beyond all this, exploration into space was opening up
new boundaries, and the decade came to an end with men walking on the
moon. They were heady days, and one could feel almost intoxicated by the
conviction that the Spirit was alive and abroad in the world, challenging our
attitudes and transforming situations before our very eyes.

But as the 1960s gave way to the 1970s, and the 1970s to the 1980s and
1990s, this optimism and excitement seemed to wane and, certainly in
Britain, there was a sense of defeat and disillusion, of sadness that the new era
of justice and peace had not materialised and instead we had voted in an era
of selfishness, of nationalism and of materialism. Ideals seemed to be

somehow quaint, not in touch with the real world and unable to be financially quantified and sold. Far better to concentrate upon obtaining a secure home-base, a stake in the share-holding society, and qualifications to ensure work in a society in which work was becoming a more and more precious commodity. 'Trickle down' theories of justice were the ones to be taken seriously, and gradually the Church, along with other institutions, became more and more concerned with its own interests and agenda, and the flame of hope and the excitement of exploration and transformation became more and more anachronistic in a society in which more and more things were deemed to be measurable and in which financial value was seen to be the most important yardstick.

Fortunately for us, the Christian Church is a universal fellowship, and whilst we were heading towards stagnation and self-preoccupation, elsewhere the Spirit was active, challenging structures, finding new meanings and keeping alive the vision of peace and justice, of hope and expectation. Nations found new freedoms (and new difficulties and temptations to go with such freedoms), apartheid was formally dismantled, the 'bias to the poor' was being explored and celebrated in smaller countries, and 'liberation' was found to be consonant with 'theology' in ways which mystified, challenged and stirred the Church in the West – or parts of the Church in the West.

The wheel is still turning, and as the 1990s draw to an end there is, I believe, a new stirring in the churches in Britain, a new awakening to theological exploration, and a new challenge to our understanding of discipleship and mission. Once again the Spirit speaks to us from the most unexpected of places, and Christ comes to us in a new guise, and calls to us from a new poor and broken, from a new experience of powerlessness, and from the cry of the person with dementia.

I met up with a friend recently who now lives in Nicaragua. His life is devoted to working alongside the poor, and we met and spoke about the challenge of community development in the poor and squalid areas of his newly adopted country. He spoke of the lack of educational opportunities, the shortage of work, the seeming impossibility of a lasting sense of justice. We spoke about exploitation, about poverty, violence and the essential nature of hope. I warmed to his descriptions of the work he was doing, and felt slightly guilty that here was 'real Christian mission and service', whilst I remained back in Britain almost cosseted by the trappings of western bourgeois society. He then asked me about what I was doing, and I talked about work with people with dementia and he told me that his mother had died recently and that she had had Alzheimer's disease for several years. He spoke to me of his inability to communicate with her, of his sense of distance and powerlessness, and it slowly became clear that dementia was another form of poverty, of powerlessness and of alienation and that it stood alongside the conditions which he was working with in a very similar and dramatic way. We were both working on the frontiers of mission, in work which clearly could be identified with Matthew 25: 14–30 ('In as much as you did it for the least of my brethren, you did it for me').

Working with people with dementia, the large majority of whom will be elderly, is slowly changing from being a backwater of social care, left behind by all the competent and exciting people, who saw it as a brake on their career progress. It is increasingly being seen as one of the most creative and challenging areas of concern, and it is attracting attention from an increasing number of researchers, professionals and funders. (Although it is still the case that for every person diagnosed as having Alzheimer's disease £10 is spent on research, as compared with £475 spent on every case of cancer which has been diagnosed and with the £15,000 spent on each case of AIDS which has been diagnosed.) At the same time it is posing new questions for the churches to consider and it is challenging accepted theological positions and requiring us to think again about a whole range of issues. It is offering us the challenge of demonstrating whether we are a people of hope, or whether we only have hope when the going is good. When confronted by issues like dementia can we discover vision, hope and words of transformation and transfiguration, or do we stand silent, unable to comprehend the scale and scope of the problem and the pain, and with nothing positive to offer?

Challenging Questions

The Church is now facing some searching and searing questions. I find that, despite over 30 years of ordained ministry, I am having to start from scratch on a whole number of issues; it is as though I have not been prepared for or taught about the world of dementia. It is therefore exciting and stimulating, and I am discovering once again some of the freshness and expectation that I encountered in the 1960s. For all who are involved in dementia care – welcome to a new journey of theological exploration and discovery!

Of all the verses in scripture, the ones which I think apply most graphically to the situation we have when thinking about dementia are those from Psalm 137: 'By the waters of Babylon we sat down and wept when we remembered thee, O Sion ... how shall we sing the Lord's song in a strange land?' The experience of dementia is certainly a strange and new land for those who suffer from it, and for their carers – they too are entering into a new, strange land, and there are very real questions about how we, and they, can sing the Lord's song in this new situation.

When anyone suffers from a physical illness there is always the possibility of there being a cure for it, and healing taking place, or if there is no cure, there is the possibility of the person coming to terms with it and in some way being able to accept it. That is another form of healing. It doesn't always happen of course, but there is always the possibility, and we approach illness with that frame of mind. In my experience many people grow spiritually through this process. This is not to encourage illness in order that people might grow, but to recognise that many people, when faced with ultimate questions and with coming to terms with an illness which is terminal do, seemingly, often in some miraculous sort of way, appear to be able to accept it and live with it, so that although the illness may conquer their body, it does not conquer their spirit. But this is not the case with dementia. People cope with loss in different ways; it may affect their personality, but it does not necessarily do so. But with dementia the very person seems to change. This raises basic questions, which have a spiritual dimension, such as 'Who am I?' and 'Which is the real me?'

When a person becomes ill with dementia we don't usually have to go very far before some basic religious questions are asked. First is usually the classic one: 'Is this a punishment from God?' We need to state with all the conviction possible that it is not. God does not will people to suffer in this way, and it would be a strange sort of God who randomly chose people and brought such havoc to their lives. The nature of the God whom we proclaim is one of love, acceptance and forgiveness and not one of cruelty, punishment or fecklessness. The second question which is often raised is: 'Is this a result of previous sin?' Once again we need to be able to give a resounding 'no' to such a suggestion. Having said that, there has to be a small caveat, in that some people may have difficulty in feeling any sense of forgiveness or acceptance because of something previously unresolved in their life. This is not the same as saying that past sin has caused dementia, but there may occasionally be cases where peace and contentment escape people because of unresolved issues. These of course may not be connected to 'sin', but they may be issues which need to be talked through and 'exorcised'. This is where skilled reminiscence work can be of great value. Finally, there comes that question, asked by so many people in so many different situations, 'How can there be a loving God, when people suffer in this way?' Whilst we may not be able to answer such a question in an intellectually satisfying manner, it *is* possible to surround and support people and their carers with a quality of love and service that enables the question to be asked in a different way. Although these are old questions, they are still asked, and we need to ensure that we are able to answer them in the context of dementia care.

The Challenge to our Theological Models

One of the greatest challenges that dementia poses to theology is that it requires us to look again at the theological model that we operate on. By that, I mean that we are challenged to state quite clearly just what our Gospel is. Can we summarise in not more than 20 words what the essence of the Gospel is – for us, and for people with dementia? The challenge of doing this forces us to look again at the presuppositions that we bring to discussions about faith.

Traditional/historical model

Most of us have probably been brought up on what I would call the traditional/historical model. In this approach the role of memory is of crucial importance. We stress the Judaeo-Christian tradition, we build upon historical events and we base our faith and our believing upon what has happened. 'I am the God of Abraham, Isaac and Jacob'; the recollection of God's saving acts in history are of great importance, and the Old Testament is full of calls to remember what God has done, how He brought the people of Israel out of the slavery of Egypt. This sense of history is carried on into the New Testament, and we are urged to 'do this in remembrance of me', in the central act of Christian worship. This model of placing great importance upon memory is taken up by the churches as they urge us to reflect upon what has happened, to have faith, to believe and to repent. We are thus required to know about the One in whom we are to have faith, to remember what it is that we are required to believe, and to remember what it is that we need to repent of – all things which are remarkably difficult for the person with dementia to do in any systematic or sustained way. Thus it would appear that the approach to faith that requires so much memory is problematic for people with dementia, and can therefore hardly be described as 'Good News'.

Open to God model

Another view about faith which some people hold is that what is important is that men and women are open to God, and that they allow themselves to be influenced by the Spirit so that they slowly, imperceptibly almost, move towards the distant horizon of God. It is the image that we find in 2 Corinthians 3–4 in which we look into a mirror and see not our own reflection, but that of Christ. It is as though we are involved in the gradual divinisation of the world, and this progression happens but can be hampered or thwarted by our own egos, by our self-will and our concern for ourselves. But such a view is not very good news for those with dementia, for their world is narrowing, and their egos seem to become more important and dominating as they lose many of their social restraints. Such a Gospel places demands upon them which most of them are quite unable to meet, and so the model, which has much to commend it in a sophisticated world, loses its power when brought into contact with the world of dementia.

Growth model

Another theological model which some people use is to see our spiritual life as a kind of parallel to our 'ordinary' life. It suggests that just as children need to grow up, and as they do so they expand their network of relationships and they develop social skills – so similarly in our spiritual life we begin as mere babes and slowly develop and grow in faith and in discipleship. We learn to grow more Godlike, it is a lifelong process of growing nearer to God. It is as though our spiritual life were a 'dialogue with God', and the interaction of that dialogue influences and shapes our spiritual growth in the same way that our interaction with other people moulds and develops the people that we become. Such a model is easy to understand and we can see very clear parallels between the two aspects of growth; it is quite a helpful model, but it makes little sense to the person with dementia. For them, their world is diminishing, not opening up, and if we are to equate spiritual growth with growth in relationships and relationship skills, then how do we deal with the experience of dementia in which relationships dwindle, and may be forgotten, and social skills decrease? It is not 'Good News' for the person with dementia.

Remembered by God model

The only theological model which seems to encapsulate the 'Good News' for the person with dementia is that which stresses the basic truth that we are 'remembered by God' long before, and long after we make any recognisable response to God. We are unconditionally accepted by God, and we are unconditionally acceptable to God. God's love and mercy, God's grace and care are not dependent upon who we are, upon what we have done, upon what we are doing or thinking at the moment, and are certainly not dependent upon any works of ours – whether physical works or 'works of faith' such as statements of belief. We are accepted. Now this is surely 'Good News' to the person with dementia. God's love is not dependent upon our memories of His mercy and love; it is not dependent upon our contrition and repentance, upon a sense of thankfulness or even upon a sense of holiness or majesty. God's love is there, to be experienced, freely and unreservedly. It is not even dependent upon acts of faith on our part – it is there – and it is there for people with dementia who may have forgotten what they believed (or disbelieved), who may have forgotten past mercies and blessings, who may have forgotten the great stories of our faith and tradition. But God is not to be bound by the limitations which illness imposes upon people, and so the 'Good News' is that there is a Gospel for people with dementia, which requires nothing from them, for God has taken all the initiatives and bears all the responsibilities. It is enough for the person just to be, and to be as they are, not as they were or as they would like to have been, but just as they are.

The Challenge to the Local Church

Dementia poses a challenge to any local church, in that Christian communities have to work out how they can best minister to people with dementia, and also to their carers. The needs of carer and cared for are both important, and they are not identical. There is a real danger that people with dementia gradually lose contact with the worshipping community; perhaps their attendance begins to drop off, and before too long we suddenly discover that Mrs Brown has not been with us for six months or even longer. Clergy (in particular) and lay leaders can then feel guilty about not having missed her, and when they do get round to visiting they find it quite difficult to have a satisfactory visit, and before too long, although she is being visited on a regular basis 'in theory', in practice the visits become fewer and fewer. Families may also be a little embarrassed by the behaviour of the person with dementia, and they often make comments that although Mrs Brown hasn't been to church for ages she doesn't really seem to miss it, as she doesn't know where she is. I have also had it explained to me that there is really no point in visiting anymore.

There have been times when I have reached the same conclusion – and I am ashamed of myself! I actually believe that it is always worth visiting, and I believe that it is extremely important that the Church remains in regular contact with people with dementia, and that we endeavour to communicate with them, hear their voice, and 'be' with them. I also know that it is sometimes extremely difficult to match such a theoretical conviction with a plan of action. Churches need help in learning how to minister to people with dementia; they need help when the person is still able to get to church, but may sometimes act and speak in what are seen to be inappropriate ways; they need help to establish good practices of home visiting and they need help in knowing how best to minister within a residential setting such as a nursing home or hospital. The fact that such ministry is difficult should not be allowed to be an excuse for not doing it.

To embark upon such a ministry, is, in fact, to discover afresh what all ministry should be, at its heart. Sheila Cassidy, in the Introduction to her book *Sharing the Darkness: The Spirituality of Caring*, writes about the 'prophetic nature' of caring for those people who in worldly terms are seen to be 'uneconomic'. She says that it is:

> a lavishing of precious resources, our precious ointment, on the handicapped, the insane, the rejected and the dying that most clearly reveals the love of Christ in our times. It is this gratuitous caring, this unilateral declaration of love, which proclaims the gospel. (Cassidy 1988, p.2)

We must see such ministry as being crucial and central to the life of our churches and not see it as a burdensome fringe activity that we undertake out of a sense of obligation. Perhaps this should be the priority in our ministry, and the mainstream work should be fitted in when we have attended to this – it's a thought. Again Cassidy puts her finger on it when she says, 'it is a particular form of Christian madness that seeks out the broken ones, the insane, the handicapped and the dying and places before their astonished eyes a banquet normally reserved for the whole and the productive'.

Such a ministry needs to be shared with the person with dementia, and this means allowing the person to participate as much as possible. The prevailing wisdom in much dementia care is that it is not really possible to hear the voice of the person with dementia, and that decisions have to be made on their behalf, by others. Such a view is now being challenged, and it seems that in many cases, though possibly not in all, the person with dementia is actually able to reflect on their situation, have views and preferences, and express them. Hearing this voice is not easy, but once again we must guard against failing to take seriously and explore something on the grounds that it is very difficult and we may not succeed. There is a growing amount of evidence to suggest that people with dementia are able to communicate to a much greater degree than has hitherto been thought possible. It surely becomes Christian ministry to be at the forefront of such patient and skilled work.

For people responsible for organising worship in residential homes and similar situations there is now a growing amount of material (albeit somewhat provisional) which explores some of the basic 'ground rules' and highlights some of the possible pitfalls. Important in this process is that the people responsible for the worship should have someone to whom they can turn to discuss their ideas and to review the worship sessions. This is important because almost built in to the very essence of such worship can be the sense that we have not quite 'got it right'. It is an area fraught with the possibilities of feeling a failure, and an outsider's view and support can be an essential ingredient in the whole planning and review procedure.

Some Fundamental Questions

Let me begin to draw to a close by opening up one or two fundamental questions which we need to explore at some length and depth from a theological perspective. I believe that there is a great deal more work to do in these areas, and they will probably be on our agendas for at least the next decade. The first concerns what it means to be human. We are only now beginning to explore the nature of personhood in the context of dementia. But in the discussions that I have come across so far any specific theological dimension seems to be lacking. Just what is happening to a person when they have dementia, and how does our doctrine of humanity cope with this process? It is all about what is a person, and who is a person.

When a person has dementia is it true to say that the person that we once knew has disappeared – and if so, where to? Personally I don't believe that this is an appropriate way forward, but if we are not going to allow that approach, then what do we have to put in its place? What has happened to the person that we knew: has their personality been destroyed or is it locked away in some as yet inaccessible part of the brain? Which is the real person –

the person as they are now, or the person that they were before their illness? I believe that there are many questions which need to be addressed here.

The second fundamental area that needs to be looked at again is the whole theology of death and dying. When does a person actually die, and what do we mean by such a word? There is a clear medical view – well, not so clear, as it now turns out. We are able to speak of being 'brain-dead', yet still breathing, and there is current debate about the ethics of switching off people's life-support machines. What about the person with advanced dementia: are they dead or alive? This is a serious question.

The mother of a friend of mine, a fellow priest, had been in a persistent vegetative state for six or seven years. She never spoke, never showed any glimmer of recognition, had to be fed and toileted; in fact had no abilities of her own and just lay in bed in a foetal position for year upon year. My friend took the view that his mother had died several years ago. But still he visited, and he said once, at a public meeting, that what he would have liked to have done was kiss his mother goodbye and place a pillow over her face. He genuinely believed that that would have been the loving and merciful thing to do. He said that she was already dead, but was still breathing. I often challenged him on this view, arguing that we just do not know what is going on in someone's brain, and expressing the view that perhaps she was still there, locked into her illness in a way which left her utterly powerless and trapped. He could not accept such a view. Following the meeting at which he spoke, two people came to see me during the next month. One of them came to express her shock and dismay that a Christian minister could express such outrageous views – did he not believe in the soul – did he not believe that God was still there and would take his mother when the time was right? The person was upset and dismayed, and said she was just thankful that she didn't attend his church. The other person came to tell me how utterly relieved she was that she had heard a priest say such words, for that was exactly how she felt and she had been harbouring feelings of immense guilt because of them. To hear that her experience was not unique and that others could understand her feelings was a sheer gift.

I do not use this illustration to argue the case for euthanasia, although I am sure that the Church needs to be aware of current thinking in this area, but to open up a theological discussion about living and dying. Is it reasonable and adequate to say that we die the moment our heart stops beating, or do we need a wider and more sophisticated view of death?

The Relevance of Theology

And so the wheel has come full circle, and as I move towards retirement in a few years' time, I am discovering afresh the importance and relevance of theology. I am sensing that in coming to grips with the illnesses which cause dementia and in endeavouring to stand alongside those who have them, and in recognising the journey that they (and their carers) are having to make, we are once again being challenged to find a word of hope for the powerless. Theology is being hammered out on the anvil of experience, and the churches are being asked if they have any 'Good News', any Gospel for these, 'the least of my brethren'.

CHAPTER 15

Some Spiritual and Ethical Issues in Community Care for Frail Elderly People

A Social Work View

Phyllida Parsloe

I intend to select a few of the many issues which I think are particularly relevant for ministers of religion and their congregations to consider.

The focus is upon older people who need help to live their daily lives, and to a lesser extent upon those who care for them. So I am writing mainly about people over 80; many will be living alone or with an elderly husband or wife but some will be living with relatives, especially daughters or sons. More will be women, since women tend to live longer than men, and many will be frail, since the older we get the more frail we are likely to become, both physically and mentally. Once we are over 80 one in every five of us will suffer from dementia. The carers will be men and women. It is widely believed that most carers are women and of these most are daughters. While many daughters are carers, in fact more spouses are the main carer and, of them, half will be husbands.

Who is Responsible for Older People who Need Care?

There is considerable confusion both about who actually is responsible and in what circumstances, as well as ethical and political questions about who ought to be.

The present policies were brought in by the National Health Service and Community Care Act 1989, which was fully implemented in 1993. The Act separated health care from social care in a way which denies the reality of human needs and which has led to many petty and distressing border disputes between hospitals and local authorities. How these are resolved has major implications for service users and their families, not least in the financial sphere, since health care is free at the point at which it is received, whilst social care is means tested. Such a division is neither logical nor ethical but seems likely to remain a complicating factor in what are already complex human situations.

The Act gave the lead responsibility for the assessment of need for community care to Local Authority Social Services departments. The guidance which accompanied the Act was contradictory. It stated that the purpose of the reforms was to empower service users and their carers. At the same time local authorities were instructed to decide upon the quality of life which was to be provided, from public funds, for those in need and also to decide on the level of needs which were to be met according to the availability of resources. This juxtaposing of choice by service users with rationing by local authorities clearly shows the clash of philosophies which occur, not only in the Act and its guidance, but in the daily lives of those who need services and the staff who assess need and provide care. Ministers and congregations will be well aware that amongst their membership and within their local communities are some elderly people with needs for care which are met only in part, or sometimes not at all.

This situation has always existed and was present even during the 1950s and 1960s when Britain could claim to have had a welfare state, although during the period it received little publicity. But since 1974 a number of changes have made the issue of care much more prominent. These include the increasing number of very elderly people both in absolute terms and as a percentage of the population, the growth of the New Right with its individualistic ideology, followed, as it now has been, by New Labour, which has accepted some of the implications of this approach, and rising expectations of health and social care. Together these have focused attention on the question of where responsibility for those who are unable to care unaided for themselves lies and where it should lie.

This is one of the major ethical questions of our time but it is seldom debated head on. Yet it would seem to be a matter which ministers and congregations must address. Does the duty of care lie with the State to which we all contribute through our taxes? If it does then how far does this duty extend? Is the State to provide a residual safety net to prevent only the most extreme form of hardship or should the State attempt to provide some kind of average standard of care. Does the idea of lesser eligibility which governed the nineteenth-century Poor Law apply? If so, are the levels of care to be held down to that which the lowest paid could afford?

But maybe the State should not provide care or at least not most of the large amount of care that is needed. In that case where, if anywhere, does the duty of care lie? It seems clear to me that Christians have a duty of care to their neighbours and some Christian teaching would suggest that the standard of care we offer others should be the best we can afford and as good as that we would want to provide for ourselves. This is what the Good Samaritan did.

Should Christians be Good Samaritans to all kinds of people? We know little about the man who fell among thieves. I have always assumed he was innocent and unfortunate. But suppose he were actually a thief himself and had outwitted the thieves who attacked him in an earlier encounter. Or suppose he had been warned about the danger of the route and told to wait for company and a daylight journey but had obstinately set off. Would and should the Good Samaritan have acted in the same way? Are we as Christians required to help others, whatever their behaviour?

We know that the Good Samaritan was not related to the man who fell among thieves. This suggests that Christian teaching requires that our care for others goes beyond those to whom we are related or with whom we share a common culture or religion. But the Good Samaritan lived in what was a relatively small world where communication went at the pace at which men and animals could travel. Now we live as part of a global community and every day we hear, almost as they are happening, of tragedies in all parts of the world. How far should our caring go and how can each human being encompass so much suffering and find a way to respond to it?

The readers of this chapter will be better equipped to answer these questions than I am. All I am doing is to suggest that these questions and others like them need to be addressed by all of us and in such a way that we can hear the many different views which are likely to be held by any collection of people.

Questions about the appropriate source of care and the nature of care have answers which have been formed over our lives and tend to be deeply and fiercely held. They have been described as 'habits of the heart' by some American sociologists (see, for example, Baldock and Ungerson 1994) and they need to be explored in two ways by those who provide care. The providers need to understand their own, often unexpressed, views. They also need to understand how those who are receiving care view it. Some people have grown old with strong beliefs in the responsibility of the State to provide care, and find receiving care from other sources demeaning. Others will have no problem in receiving charitable help and may find help from voluntary organisations more acceptable than help from the local authority. Others may feel that only by paying can they maintain their dignity as human beings.

A recent study (Baldock and Ungerson 1994) also showed that people can buy for themselves or accept from providers some kinds of care but not others. Some elderly people have no difficulty in accepting, or spending their savings on, consumer goods like washing machines or even stairlifts. They have bought such equipment all their lives. But if they are asked to contribute towards the cost of personal care this may be quite outside the habits of a lifetime.

Similarly, who provides the care may be very important. Studies have shown that older people can, albeit sometimes very reluctantly, accept personal care from close female relatives or from paid staff. They would find it unacceptable if a volunteer came to bath them and many would be appalled if male relatives took on certain forms of care.

I have gone beyond the ethical and political questions into the details which anyone receiving or offering care needs to address. These details are practical but they must be addressed if we are to provide services which are acceptable to our fellow citizens who need care and if services are not to demean them as fellow human beings. If we venture into the dangerous territory of helping others we have a moral responsibility to consider the meaning of our intervention to those who receive our help.

Who Provides the Care

I have already mentioned that, unlike most health care, social care is not free at the point of delivery. Financial assessments of both income and capital are made and users may be charged for the services which the social services staff have decided they need.

This leads to some very difficult situations, especially when the potential service users refuse to pay. Many want to protect all of their savings, either for a rainy day or to pass on to children. The social services staff are in a dilemma. They have assessed the elderly man or woman as needing services and, given the levels at which need is recognised, only serious need will be assessed as requiring provision. Then the user will not pay. Should the local authority withdraw the service? The treasurer's department may well say 'yes', but the staff providing the service will be very concerned at leaving a fellow citizen without help. Sometimes staff continue to provide help but in doing so they put themselves at risk of disciplinary action.

Local councils and those who vote them into power, which is you and I, need to ask what policy the authority follows in such situations. Then we have to decide whether or not we can support it. If we cannot, then, as individuals and as congregations, we need to make our views known.

Assessment and Spiritual Needs

The National Health Service and Community Care Act require local authorities to carry out an assessment of anyone who appears to need some services. In fact local authorities have developed different levels of assessment so that not everyone who, for example, asks for a bath rail, is the subject of a full assessment. Nevertheless, many full assessments are carried out by local authority staff, often with assistance from medical and nursing staff as well. The assessment is meant to cover medical, social, financial and emotional needs. What is not included are spiritual needs.

There is an important and neglected role here for ministers and congregations. So far as I am aware there are no local authority social services departments which have ministers attached to them as spiritual advisers for staff and service users. Prisons and hospitals do, and chaplains in these services clearly deal with spiritual as well as religious matters when working with prisoners, patients and relatives. Why, I wonder, are there no chaplains available to help in the assessment which leads to a care plan by the local authority? I know, of course, that ministers are sometimes incidentally involved where the person being assessed is a member of their congregation, but it is not only those with religious beliefs who have spiritual needs.

One might argue that social workers should be able to help their clients to talk about spiritual needs and help them find ways to meet them. Perhaps this will happen in time but my experience of social workers is that, at least once they are trained, they seldom raise spiritual questions and I suspect that they sometimes make it difficult for clients to raise them.

I fear that history and training has something to do with this inappropriate denial of spiritual needs by social services. The State social services are still, to an extent, running away from their religious past. One of the strands from which present-day social services developed was the religious voluntary societies of the late nineteenth century. These societies were often engaged in evangelical activities as well as social services. Social workers today are at pains to reject this part of their history. In doing so they confuse spirituality, religion and evangelism and, to be on the safe side, avoid all three.

Sadly, their professional training plays into this rejection. I have noticed over the years that spiritual matters and religious concerns seem to have been taboo topics on the university social work courses for which I have been responsible. No one talked about such matters and my academic colleagues never told each other about their own beliefs although all other areas seemed to be openly discussed. When I gave introductory talks to incoming students I mentioned my own religious beliefs and almost every year some student or colleague commented on this and told me how brave I was. The bravery, I surmised, was in risking being labelled as a do-gooding evangelist.

I wondered whether students had been freer to discuss spiritual matters before they started training. I sent a questionnaire to 40 students in 1996 asking them four questions:

1. Had they discussed spiritual matters with clients before they came on the course?

2. Had they discussed them with clients during fieldwork placements on the course?

3. Had they discussed them with fellow students and staff on the course?

4. Did they think it appropriate for social workers to talk with clients about spiritual matters?

The results were clear and very worrying. Almost all those replying (about 90 per cent) answered 'yes' to questions 1 and 4 and 'no' to questions 2 and 3.

The questionnaires were anonymous but I asked at the end whether the respondent would be willing to talk to me. Six said they would and gave their names. I met three as a group and the other three individually. What became clear was that in fact these students had found each other and now talked about spiritual matters with each other, but not when in groups with other students. They had a shared view of what spirituality was; for them it was a search for the meaning of life and the nature of death. They felt that social work had suffered from confusing religion and spirituality and all were adamant that they would never attempt to convert a client. That would be morally wrong and an abuse of their privileged position which allowed them to come close into other people's lives.

I speculated with these students, all of whom were women, as to why social workers seem so reluctant to discuss spiritual matters with colleagues or clients. They agreed that social work history was a factor. We also wondered whether social workers were avoiding facing the question of what the purpose of life is. We thought that there is a real difficulty in facing this question with very elderly people who feel they have nothing to offer and who can see no purpose in life. It may be even harder to face with the relatives of those suffering from dementia. In our society it is hard to find an answer. Purposes in life are connected with doing and not with being. The Christian emphasis upon giving contributes to the difficulty. If it is really more blessed to give than to receive, then where does that leave some dependent elderly people?

Perhaps churches need not only to address the issue of reciprocity, of giving and receiving rather than just giving, but also to consider whether the idea that it is more blessed to give than to receive needs to be put into the context of a lifetime, so that we develop a chronology of reciprocity across a lifespan. We have no difficulty in children being receivers and perhaps we could accept for ourselves, as well as others, that the end as well as the beginning of life is a time when one may receive more than one can give. The balance can be provided in the middle years.

We may also need to work hard at finding ways in which older people, and especially those over 75 years of age, can give as well as receive. In earlier times older people (although few lived to be over 75) were a source of advice and wisdom. It is clearly false to think that all old people were wise. Presumably some, like those in other age groups, may well have been opinionated or stupid, but the general belief in the wisdom of age may have given older people a place in society and a status. Our fast changing technological age tends to see older people as out of date and they feel this themselves and lose confidence as a result. However, there are matters, such as relationships between people, which do not change in the same way as technology does and upon which older people have at least as good a grip as younger ones.

Some recent research (Baltes and Baltes 1986) supports this view. It was generally believed that older people became slower and less able to take decisions or give advice. It is now being shown that while old people reach decisions more slowly than do younger people, they actually take more factors into account and use life experience in solving problems. They can handle more complex situations without foreclosing the decision. So there may be a psychological base for the belief in the wisdom of old age. Of course, not every old person has such capacity for wisdom but the recognition that the idea of intelligence has been unduly limited to the narrow ability of solving problems fast may create a more receptive climate for reciprocity between old and younger people.

Carers and Service Users

One of the most serious ethical issues facing those involved in care in the community is that what service users want and what those family members, neighbours and friends who care for them want, may conflict. The guidance on the 1989 National Health Service and Community Care Act (Department of Health 1991) does not recognise this nor is it fully acknowledged in more recent legislation. Government policy is intended to allow as many people as possible to remain in their own homes for as long as possible. There are dangers in such a policy. Carers may suffer since it is they and not the state who usually provide the bulk of the caring, and providing long-term intensive care can be an isolating and demanding experience for some. It might not be what the carer would choose were other options available. It can also put the user at risk. Being cared for at home may mean long periods alone, being frightened by pain or by insecurity, managing the anxieties of ageing alone and being dealt with by harassed relatives who may be angry or even physically abusive.

In assuming a shared interest between user and carer, the Act and its guidance have obscured the reality of daily life and have failed to balance the need for autonomy with the need for protection. In the long run the latter omission may prove to have been beneficial. It at least corrected a tendency to do things to older people as if they were no longer responsible for themselves. However, it may now be time to reassess the balance.

Competence in Older People

The law is in a state of confusion about competence in adults but, even if the Law Commission's sensible suggestions are finally implemented, there will still be difficult decisions to make. In part this is because competence and incompetence are not completely separate states. Older people, like younger people, are likely to be more competent when they are feeling secure, are in good health, have slept well and are not anxious. Competence can fluctuate and does so even amongst those suffering from dementia. The way in which those who help approach older people can have a major effect upon their competence. Giving time is of great importance and so is being active in seeking out the views of older people. Kitwood and his colleagues (Kitwood and Bredin 1992) have suggested that the physical effects of dementia are compounded by the way in which people behave to those who are sufferers. When we are with someone without dementia and they use the wrong name or speak sentences which do not seem to follow on from each other, we would point out what was happening and give the speaker the chance to try again or explain the connection. Not so with a dementia sufferer. We begin to treat them as different and they can feel this happening. Their own identity, which is already threatened by the dementia, is further undermined by unnatural and unreal responses from friends and relatives. Such behaviour is really the non-verbal equivalent of lying and, although the intention is to be helpful, the results may be destructive.

Some of the information about what dementia sufferers feel comes from them themselves. Increasingly, people are being told that their diagnosis is, say, Alzheimer's disease. For a time doctors felt unable to do this but now many are able to do so and there are benefits. In some areas, counselling services are available for those who have received such a diagnosis. Counselling can provide some human support with the horrifying implications of the diagnosis and also help to pre-plan for a future when competence is lost. It is enormously helpful to carers to know that when they have to make decisions about care in the future, they do not just guess that 'this is what he would have wanted', but actually know – 'he said he wanted this to happen.'

Sharing the diagnosis, counselling and pre-planning are ways of ensuring that dementia sufferers have a say in their own care and are listened to. This eases the difficult ethical questions which arise when one adult has to act in the best interest of another adult.

The Role of Congregations

In the United States some recent research (Cnaan 1997) seems to show that with the cutbacks in State-provided welfare, religious congregations are moving into the gap produced. They do this in a number of ways:

1. By collecting money and giving it to various voluntary welfare agencies.

2. By individual members of the congregation serving as volunteers on a great range of different welfare programmes, run by the State, voluntary agencies and private providers.

3. By groups in the congregation running services themselves.

4. By allowing their often extensive buildings to be used, either for a fee or free, by a range of State, voluntary, self-help and private welfare agencies.

5. By joining in local and national protests about welfare issues.

I have just started to undertake a similar study in the Bristol area and the same five types of services are all present there although the scale of giving money and of running services (1 and 3 above) is smaller than in the US study. This, however, may be explained by the fact that the State welfare services in the UK are still much more extensive than in the US. In talking to volunteers who are also members of religious congregations, I have the impression that volunteering is part of their contribution, as Christians, to the well-being of their neighbours, but is not directly related to being a member of a particular congregation. The use of buildings is apparent in Bristol, but the interesting thing about this is that until I actually ask the questions the ministers very seldom volunteer this information, since they have not thought of it as a contribution to social welfare.

I have not done enough yet to be able to say what the role of congregations is in relation to social welfare, let alone what Christian congregations should be doing. So I leave that question with readers.

CHAPTER 16

Spirituality, Ageing and Gender

Ursula King

Spirituality is a much discussed topic today, but what does it mean? There are so many definitions and different understandings of it that a person enquiring about spirituality can easily get puzzled by the numerous answers on offer. The variety of advice now available is truly confusing. Spirituality certainly has to do with life and living, with certain attitudes and practices, but judging from so many current publications, conferences and activities, spirituality has now also become a new academic discipline which can be studied, even explored as a field of 'global spirituality'. Yet it is not these new academic developments which concern me here, but rather the meaning of spirituality within the context of ageing. Over the years I have written much on spirituality in a general sense until I became aware that gender variables, together with other differentiating factors which shape the pattern of our lives, are an important consideration for the understanding and practice of spirituality.

We can expand and deepen the meaning of spirituality by relating spiritual advice and practical help to the concrete life situation of particular people, both the old and the young. At the present time many specific ideas, based on particular experiences, act almost like searchlights with which to investigate and explore the dynamics of spiritual life in a more focused and intense manner. The experience of ageing is such a focus, and the experience of gender is another. We now already possess a growing number of studies which relate spirituality to the experience of children, for example, to the expanding life world and growth of the young. There even exists a new journal devoted to this topic, the *International Journal of Children's Spirituality*.[1]

---

1   Edited by Clive and Jane Erricker, this journal is published in Oxford by Carfax Publishing Ltd. See also the fine study of Robert Coles (1992) *The Spiritual Life of Children*, which includes examples from Jewish, Christian, Islamic and secular sources.

However, as far as I know, no corresponding publication has been developed yet for the other end of life's spectrum, for the years of maturity, diminishment and decline when our vital energies slowly disperse. The present book may therefore be a milestone signalling a new development in the searching reflections on spirituality in our contemporary world by addressing the place of spirituality in ageing.

Traditionally, many cultures have seen old age as a fountain of wisdom which the young have revered and been nourished by. Different religions have provided considerable spiritual advice on how to live a good human life, full of dignity and respect for others, and how to practise renunciation and detachment so as to prepare for a good death. Hinduism in particular knows of four stages of life where the last, in old age, prepares for full spiritual liberation, but other religions, too, contain many teachings on old age and death. But I do not think that spirituality, as we understand it today, can be deduced in full from such traditional teachings, which in any case do not pay attention to gender differences, but were always formulated as general, universal norms.

As human beings have got to know the world much more closely and studied it more carefully, they have become aware of many important differences. One such fundamental difference is that of gender, the way we understand being male and female, living as women and men with different histories, different experiences and different expectations. Critical gender studies represent a significant modern development, but they are in practice still widely equated with issues primarily raised by and concerned with women, although their true extent covers all that is human, women as well as men in all their individual and gender differences, and their similarities. However, since traditional views on spirituality, as in all other matters, have not paid any attention to the specificity of either male or female experience but have been simply imposed as universal insights (constructed on the basis of one-sided male experience alone rather than on women's and men's experience together), more work is required to bring out the specificity and difference of women's experience before one looks again at the experience of men from a new vantage point. I therefore suggest that whilst I will begin with some general remarks on spirituality, but also on spirituality and ageing (much more fully discussed by other contributors to this book), my main task will be to look especially at women and spirituality during the process of ageing.

What is Spirituality?

Numerous definitions of spirituality have been proposed. Some of these are explicitly religious, whereas others are much wider and can include interfaith as well as secular contexts. For example, Evelyn Underhill wrote that the spiritual life is 'the heart of all real religion and therefore of vital concern to ordinary men and women'; that it is 'that full and real life for which humanity is made'.[2] Here the spiritual is seen as the deepest centre and core, 'the heart' of religion, whereas other approaches focus on shared human experience and its specifically spiritual potential. Such a perspective marks spirituality as wider than the exclusively religious. For example, an earlier report of a Working Party on Spirituality set up by the Scottish Churches Council defined spirituality as 'an exploration into what is involved in becoming human', or an 'attempt to grow in sensitivity, to self, to others, to non-human creation and to God who is within and beyond this totality' (*Working Party Report on 'Spirituality'* 1973, p.3). More recently, it was suggested at a conference that spirituality means to be truly awake, to make a project out of one's life, and to consciously strive for self-integration through self-transcendence.

What these approaches have in common is the contemporary emphasis which bases our thinking about spirituality on human experience and psychology, which grounds spirituality anthropologically rather than deducing it from specific theological and religious premises. This is a new way of looking at spirituality, for traditionally theologians and writers on spirituality have always written from within a particular religious perspective and have presented spirituality as a special calling, a process and a goal rooted in the beliefs of a particular religion. In Christianity, for example, the Gospel call, 'You must be perfect as your Father in heaven is perfect' (Matthew 5:48) inspired early Christians to seek for spiritual perfection, for a life lived in the spirit of God. This command led to the development of Christian asceticism, monasticism and mysticism. Countless Christian writers, from the desert fathers and mothers to medieval and modern saints and mystics, have left us copious writings describing their spiritual quests and transformation, which provide us with numerous models of Christian holiness and discipleship.

Christianity, together with all other faiths, possesses a rich spiritual heritage which is being studied and re-appropriated with a renewed interest

---

2   See the inspiring little book by Evelyn Underhill (repr. 1993) *The Spiritual Life: Great Spiritual Truths for Everyday Life.*

today.[3] This is further enhanced by the general interest in spirituality in contemporary society, linked to the interest in the human subject and the need for profound personal and social transformation, of which many people are now acutely aware. Thus spirituality is of considerable interest to those working in psychotherapy and the human potential movement, to adherents of new religious movements, and to supporters of the ecological and peace movement as well as the women's movement. Contemporary understandings of spirituality capture the dynamic, transformative quality of spirituality as lived experience, an experience linked to our bodies, to nature, to our relationships with others and society. It is an experience which seeks the fullness of life, of a life of justice and peace, of integrating body, mind and soul, a life that touches the hem of the spirit in the midst of all our struggles of living.

Spirituality and the Process of Ageing

I deliberately use the term 'process of ageing' rather than speak of a definite stage of 'old age' (which occurred at a younger age in previous generations). Ageing is an ongoing dynamic and organic experience, for we are all involved in the process of getting older from the moment we are born, and thus ageing is a psychological as well as a biological experience. This occurs on a continuum and is given different meaning by different individuals. However, when speaking about 'ageing' here, the years after the middle of life and towards the end of life are meant, the years of retirement, after one has reached 60, 70, 80 years or more. The demographic developments in modern society are such that people are living longer and getting older all the time.

Recently a *Guardian* article (*The Guardian* 1997) reported that 30 years ago there were 271 centenarians living in the UK whereas in 1997 there were 8000, and most of these are women. Here is evidence of an important gender variable, namely that women have a longer life expectancy, and therefore they will also have specific spiritual needs in coping with such longevity. The article contained some interviews with several of these women centenarians, highlighting how their life-world had shrunk and their

3   See the important series of Christian texts published in the *Classics of Western Spirituality: A Library of Great Spiritual Masters* which has appeared since 1978 (New York: Paulist Press/London: SPCK). For excellent studies on spirituality in different world faiths see the books in the series *World Spirituality: An Encyclopedic History of the Religious Quest* published since 1985 (New York: Crossroad/London: Routledge).

activities were constrained by physical impairment, but also how much some of them retained their incredible zest and love of life. This reminded me of a recent experience when I visited a wonderful woman of the great age of 106, the oldest living person I have ever met. She lived with her daughter of 74, and both were in excellent health and exceptionally energetic, full of ideas, interests and, above all, tremendously inspiring presence. It was a great experience for me, a true moment of grace, to be in the presence of a gifted woman of 106 who was so alert and alive, so full of all her human capacities, and so interested in things of the spirit. Here were spiritual energies fully embodied in a human being, energies that spoke of the powers of life, of hope, of forceful realities stronger than any human frailty. It was a high point in my life, an unforgettable moment which challenged me more than any other to think of my own ageing as a woman, becoming acutely aware of the need to deepen this process through spiritual growth and insight.

Another inspiring experience for me was to see a recent exhibition of the life story and paintings of 'Grandma Moses' (1860–1961), the famous American woman painter who, after spending all her life on farms in New England and upstate New York where she raised numerous children and grandchildren (five of the ten children she gave birth to died in infancy), took to the creative act of painting in her early seventies, after her husband had died. She painted for more than 30 years, acquired fame and fortune, but always remained a simple rural woman. I watched several filmed interviews in which she expressed her views on life and art, conveying a wonderful, humble presence, radiating her deep love for nature and life. There are no explicitly religious motifs in her paintings of landscapes, family occasions, seasonal festivals and bucolic life close to earth, yet her whole work is suffused with a spiritual quality, with what in another context has been called 'the transfiguration of the ordinary', an expression of something luminous, joyful and of great beauty.

The experiences made me reflect more intensely on the question: what are the spiritual needs of people getting older? What resources are available to them for developing greater spiritual strength and succour in times of need? Where are fresh horizons of hope when the light of life is waning? And what special spiritual needs may women have when living longer and alone?

Women, Spirituality and Ageing

Spirituality is an important theme in the contemporary women's movement, and many older women are deeply involved with explorations into and experiments with spirituality through meditation and art, through work in groups, through different rituals, creative encounters and nourishing friendships. Sometimes this explicit interest in spirituality among contemporary women is described as womanspirit movement or as spiritual feminism (in contrast to political, liberal, and secular feminism). But in addition to this explicit pursuit of spiritual themes there also exists an implicit spiritual dimension in the feminist movement, for the goals of women's liberation, peace and justice, of seeking the full humanity of women, are not only social, economic and political aims, but are ultimately spiritual aims, as I have argued in my book *Women and Spirituality, Voices of Protest and Promise* (King 1993). Women have turned away from the traditional, dualistic sense of spirituality where body, world and matter were divided from the world of the spirit. Instead, they understand spirituality as a search for wholeness and integration, for transformation and celebration. Their new understanding of spirituality provides a fundamental critique of traditional patriarchal attitudes to gender, work, the environment and other aspects of life.

In seeking freedom from oppression in all its forms, in working for their own liberation and the full humanity of all people, women today are in search of the integration of all their experiences. This includes the search for inclusiveness, connectedness and mutuality, for embodiment and concreteness, so that we can be truly at home – in our bodies, in our society, in the universe.

It is from such a new, transformative and integral vision of spirituality that women now speak and write about spirituality. One such writer emphasises that spirituality should not be seen as a series of fixed stages but rather as the dynamic steps of a dance, moving backwards and forwards as well as upwards. In that sense the dance of spirituality intertwines with the whole dance of life, and it is this dynamic movement that we women of an older generation can see unfolding in all its richness. Another movement is not unlike that suggested to the young, namely 'exploring life's possibilities' through both 'looking inwards' and 'looking outwards'.[4] The older person can do this too, but does it from a different vantage point.

By looking inwards and outwards across the years of life, women can knit together so many of their experiences and integrate them through an inner effort into a pattern and meaning of their own which can relate to the pattern and meaning of other people's lives. Older women often live on their own, or in a community with other women and men. They may have a wider family of more distant relations, or share in the joys and pains of their children and grandchildren, or they may be entirely on their own. What is most important for every woman, though for each in a different way, is the inner effort, the intention and will to reflect on the experiences of her life and see them in a larger setting. For this, the powers of the imagination and the heart have to be nourished and an openness of mind needs to be actively fostered. At a time of life when for many the powers of physical life are failing, it is essential to discover the strength and help of inner resources, together with outer ones, to seek inspiration and help for life's daily struggles and to engage with questions of one's own personal search for meaning. Here, an openness to community, to the help coming from others, whether through visits, conversation, reading, or group work, is a helpful start. But the most important work is one's own, the work of befriending our own souls and memories so as to find answers to some of our deeper longings.

Life's Struggle and the Dance of the Spirit: Some Practical Help for Women

Christian women in different parts of the so-called Third World have described spirituality as 'the struggle for life', a struggle which involves for them the freedom from oppression, the resistance to violence, but also the joy and celebration of life in all its aspects (Mary John Mananzan et al. 1996). The struggle for life is quite literally the immense labour and effort to bring human life into the world, which women uniquely do. But it is also the continuing struggle to attend to all the details of growth, to nurture life with love and care, to survive against all odds, to make ends meet, to produce the food needed for many mouths, to calm family feuds and quarrels. On a larger scale still, the struggle for life is all around us: it is the rise and persistence of life in the whole universe; it surrounds us everywhere in nature; it invades our bodies through the rhythm of life and death. If we can see the lineaments, the breath of the spirit within and throughout these struggles, then we discover a

4   *Looking inwards, looking outwards: exploring life's possibilities.* Teacher Handbook and Student resource Book (1997). Derby: The Christian Education Movement, sponsored by the John Templeton foundation.

great horizon of hope, the sustaining power of faith in the fullness of life even when experiencing physical decline.

Spirituality is then a different way of seeing – seeing our own life, that of others and all of life on earth in a different light and from a different perspective. It is the discovery of new insight and wisdom whereby we reshape the innerness of our life and reflect on the presence and help of God in the midst of all life, but especially in our own hearts. The growth of spirituality is always connected with an inner awakening, a discovery and transforming of one's understanding and insight. It is being responsive to the dance of the spirit across the struggles, the depths and heights of human life. This development can happen at any moment and any age in one's life, and there are certainly deeply spiritual people who are quite young. However, it is generally acknowledged that it is in the older, mature years of one's life, when many of one's personal struggles have been resolved and responsibilities have been lightened, at a time when one can slow down (and physically is forced to do so), that one finds more occasion for reflection, for the ingathering of life's riches and graces, and an opportunity for a deeper healing of life's painful wounds.

To be fully human is to discover the spiritual dimension of our existence, and that is possible through the experience of our bodies, through our relationships to others and to our environment, to the whole cosmos around us. The presence of the spirit can make itself known everywhere, for God may meet us at any place and any time. Such an encounter often happens especially at times of crisis which then reveal themselves as times of great graces and teach us that we can experience, celebrate and pray our spirituality in many different ways.

The spiritual needs of older women are as diverse as individual personalities and life histories are. These vary across a wide spectrum. Yet one can point to some general characteristics which affect all older women in one way or another. It is important to come spiritually to terms with oneself, with other people and one's environment, with the world at large, by developing a deeper, more accepting and appreciative understanding of all one's experiences. There is the need to acknowledge realistically one's state of health or illness, one's tiredness and diminution of physical strength. There is also the need to deal with one's loneliness, especially if one's partner has died, the need to let go many ties and relationships and to accept the world as it is, to acknowledge without grudge and judgement the different outlook and lifestyle of younger people, including that of one's own children and grandchildren. But there is also the deeper need to develop a greater, more inclusive tolerance, an acceptance of experiences which cannot be undone, forgiveness, inner peace and the nurturing of love within one's heart for all beings. Some older women have the need to pray more and seek God in all things. A traditional religious faith, whatever it is, may in fact be the strongest resource to inspire, guide and sustain people's lives, but there are also many other resources older women can draw on, within themselves and through the help of others.

At an individual level women can do meditative memory work, re-appropriating experiences of childhood, youth and adulthood and thereby reclaiming the realities of their lives, the markers of growth and pain, of loss, enrichment and joy, the fruits of different seasons. What is the deeper, inner meaning of all these experiences and events of their life? How does a woman relate to her own mother? Who are the influential women of particular significance in a woman's life? And who are our known foremothers in the pattern of life we have chosen, or our foremothers of faith from whom we can draw strength and encouragement? Women can do this kind of work in groups, sharing their experiences with other women friends and connecting with their reflections and thoughts which help them to see their own life in a different, richer light. Some women have created new rituals, prayers and liturgies of thanksgiving and celebration which arise out of their own experiences and connect with that of others. A group of older women living together in a home or meeting in a group could do this for themselves and experience a feeling of renewed strength and energy as well as gratitude for their lives. I quote a few lines from a celebration of Asian religious women:

> We celebrate today the struggle of women all over the world ... Spirit of Life, we remember today the women, named and unnamed, who throughout time have used the power and gifts you gave them to change the world. We call upon the foremothers to help us discover within ourselves your power – and the ways to use it to bring about the kingdom of Justice and Peace ... We have celebrated the power of many women past and present. It is time now to celebrate ourselves. With each of us is that same life and light and love. Within each of us lie seeds of power and glory. Our bodies can touch with love; our hearts can heal; our minds can seek our faith and truth and justice. Spirit of Life, be with us in our quest. (John Mananzan 1992, pp.206–7)

Not every woman is creative enough to found a woman's group or develop the work of inner spiritual reflection on her own. Many of these efforts are so new that we need guidance through workshops, counsellors, discussion groups or helpful books and booklets. Specialised studies and resource material on women and spirituality continue to grow, but, as mentioned at the beginning of this article, there is as yet very little material dealing with older women and their specific spiritual needs and resources. Kathleen Fischer's book *Women at the Well* (1988) contains an interesting chapter on 'Grandmothers, Mothers, and Daughters: The Spiritual Legacy', with reflections on reclaiming women's spiritual heritage across different generations, on healing the painful legacy of women's lives, and on integrating insights from motherhood into spirituality.

A much fuller treatment, which includes many ideas and practices relevant to older women, is found in a very imaginative and original book by Maria Harris, *Dance of the Spirit: The Seven Steps of Women's Spirituality* (1991). Here, the dynamic development of women's spirituality is explained through the moving steps of a dance, incorporating practical exercises of centring, awakening, remembering, discovering, celebrating and engaging with spiritual insights through the rhythms of a woman's life from youth to old age. Harris uses an inclusive understanding of spirituality as related to all of life when she writes that:

> Initially, spirituality is seeing. This means not just looking but seeing what is actually there, seeing into and entering the deep places and centres of things ... our spirituality begins with our cultivating the inner eye that sees everything as capable of being ... 'saturated with God.' (p.65)

She also distinguishes between different forms of spirituality that are contemplative, actively engaged, resisting or simply receptive. Receptivity is an integral part of life, but marks especially those who are bedridden, or palsied, or mentally unable. They are women who are ill or old, or in some way forced to be waiters and watchers, no longer able, if they ever were, to be completely involved in a physical, questioning, resisting, or empowering spirituality – although their receptivity may itself be a form of each of these. These are the women who experience life as something to be received in totality and are almost completely dependent on the care of others. They teach the rest of us much about a side of life that belongs in each of us but is too often ignored: a side of spirituality that sometimes arrives quickly, sometimes accidentally, yet eventually claims us if we live long enough ...

> At the beginning of life we are full of physical energy, but we are also in some sense almost totally receptive – waiting for life to come and meet us. At the end of our lives we are forced to be receptive, especially as we befriend death, but this is often totally determined by our physical circumstances. And in the midst of, as well as in between both physical and receptive life, we all have periods of questioning, resisting, and empowering. (Harris 1991, p.73)

Women's spirituality, as practised and discussed today, has much to do with empowering, with nourishing our hearts and souls, or with what Harris describes so aptly as the 'tending' of the garden of our spirit, a garden which must also be a dwelling place for growing old where we discover that we are capable of bearing fruit. But 'as the seasons pass and blend into one another, we find that the years let us bear a certain kind of riper and fuller fruit, not possible when we were young. These fruits are the wisdoms and insights and secrets we have culled from living through several decades, and they give us strength, a stability, and a joy that cannot be forgotten.' We also discover that 'as we have been tending, so too has Another', the Spirit of God, the Source of Life (Harris 1991, pp.96–7). This passage is reminiscent of St Teresa of Avila's homely advice about Christian prayer life which she compares to the different ways of watering a garden. Only regular watering will ensure that the plants grow to their full beauty, but by far the most effective form of watering occurs by God's own efforts through providing heavy rain.

In a more general sense these examples represent an actively engaged and interpretative spirituality which bridges and connects all the different levels and facets of life's experiences. It relates the numerous ways of being human with each other and connects them to a deeper, all-encompassing ground. I sometimes describe it as a spiritual alchemy of transformation, for such a spiritual approach is a practice and technique which can be learnt and taught, a profoundly transformative practice which helps to foster peace, contentment and happiness within oneself and in relation with others. Some women today emphasise a new, exclusively feminist spirituality which rejects links with traditional religions and instead creates spiritual resources of its own. Personally, I prefer a more integrated approach which draws on both old and new spiritual resources. The spiritual heritage of women in the different world faiths is very rich and empowering since all religious traditions and cultures know of inspiring women of spirit from whom we can learn a great deal. But we also know of many spiritually inspiring women in our own time who embody many different ways of human life, creativity and faith (see Bancroft 1989).

The most important question today is how to nourish ourselves spiritually, how to tend to and draw on precious spiritual energy resources which can feed our lives as individuals and communities, thereby helping us to live and die responsibly and with dignity. The experience of many older women can help younger ones to live such a spiritually enriched life, and many older women can be helped in their own journey into old age, into letting go and being fulfilled, by learning to apply spiritual attitudes and reflections to the wealth of human experiences inscribed in their bodies, hearts and minds.

CHAPTER 17

Spirituality and Ageing in British Hindus, Sikhs and Muslims

Shirley Firth

While physical signs of ageing are universally recognised, concepts of ageing are socially constructed and vary from culture to culture. Westernised cultures, with economic, scientific and medical advances, have to find ways of reconstructing concepts of ageing to take into account longer lives, with larger numbers of elderly than ever before, many of whom face 20 or 30 years without meaningful employment. For Hindus, Sikhs and Muslims, age is seen in the context of the whole lifespan, which is itself to be lived with a view to the final goal, life after death, whether this is understood in terms of heaven or, for Hindus and Sikhs, also includes the possibility of rebirth or liberation from the cycle of birth and death. The conceptual framework within which ageing is understood thus takes into account social, religious and spiritual dimensions to life seen as a whole, with particular obligations on senior members of society to be spiritually and practically prepared for their own demise, but also to develop wisdom and maturity which can be a guide and help to younger members of society.

Old age is a blessing from God, and for Hindus and Sikhs, an indication of their good karma[1] in a previous life. On the Indian subcontinent in the past, where life expectancy was low, there would have been comparatively few elderly people, and they were regarded as repositories of wisdom and deferred to. The joint family system provided security for the elderly although much of this is changing with better lifestyles among the middle classes, social mobility and urbanisation

---

1   Karma: literally action, is the causal law in which good deeds and bad deeds have automatic consequences for the next life, and explains the distribution of good and bad fortune in this life.

This chapter looks briefly at the religious and spiritual framework within which Hindus, Sikhs and Muslims approach ageing and death, and then focuses on individual British South Asians' perspectives on ageing within the context of life in this country, to show both the difficulties faced by many elders who are uprooted from their homelands, and the ways in which individuals have adapted and developed their spiritual and religious lives. The case studies are based on personal interviews by the writer

Scripture and Tradition

Hinduism

There is a vast body of literature in the Hindu tradition going back more than 3000 years. Until very recently, however, the Sanskrit texts were only accessible to men in the top three classes (*varnas*) (Rig Veda (R.V.) X.18.3; X.18.3–4). In the most ancient texts, the Vedic Samhitas (ca.1500–1000 BCE), the Aryan people were joyful, life-affirming and pragmatic. A life of 'a hundred full autumns' (*Rig Veda* X.18.3; 118.4) is prayed for. Death does not seem to be feared or seen as a discontinuity. Heaven is rather like this earth, ruled over by the benevolent Yama, the king of the dead, and Varuna (RV X.18.5; RV.X.16.3; X 14; AV XVIII.2; 3; 4). The ancestors have a symbiotic relationship with the living, granting long life and progeny in return for sacrifices and nourishment.

By the time of the Upanishads (ca.800–200 BCE) the emphasis on sacrifice and the concomitant Brahmin domination had begun to pall, and the tendency to mysticism and speculation glimpsed in the Vedas developed fully, along with belief in karma and reincarnation according to one's good or bad deeds. Dissatisfaction with urban life drove many men into the forest to meditate, seeking mystical enlightenment. This led to a split between their teaching and that of the Brahmins, reflected in the Upanishadic texts. Those who had concentrated on traditional rituals (the way of action) would have a good rebirth. However, those who sought mystical knowledge would not be reborn, but would become one with Brahman (*Brihadaranyaka Upanishad* 6.2.15-16; *Chandogya Upanishad* 5.10). The ageing body 'as a heavily loaded cart goes creaking ... in weakness and ... confusedness of mind' at the end of life (*Br.Up.* 4.3.35–4.4.1). 'According as one acts...so does he become. The doer of good becomes good. The doer of evil becomes evil' *(Br. Up.*4.4.5). Those who have no desire and recognise their identity with Brahman, Ultimate Reality, become Brahman (*Br. Up.* 4.4.6ff).

Siddhartha Gautama, the Buddha (b.563 BCE), had a profound influence on the development of Hindu mysticism, since he emphasised the pain and sorrow of ageing and the decay of the body which could only be overcome by following the Noble Eightfold Path to enlightenment, Nirvana. His followers became ascetics, leaving their homes and families to follow him, and the community of monks (*sangha*) evolved. It is possible that the concept of the four stages of life, the *ashramas*, developed as a reaction to this as Hinduism reasserted its hold (Tilak 1989, p.34ff.). These stages (below) allowed for the ascetic life *after* the normal duties of the householder in ensuring that the continuity of the line and of society had been fulfilled. The sacred obligations (*rna*) to society, to the gods, the seers, the natural world, the ancestors (and thus parents), and the way of righteousness within the framework of natural and moral order, are part of one's *dharma*,[2] which include caste and class (*varna*) duties. The twice-born[3] adult Hindu male, therefore, follows *varnashramadharma*; his class/caste duties, his religious and moral obligations and the appropriate stage of life. He fulfils his obligations as a householder by pursuing the three aims: *dharma*, *artha* (wealth by honest means), and *kama* (pleasure). He needs sons to perpetuate the lineage and perform funeral and ancestral rites. When he sees his grandsons he can focus on the fourth aim, *moksha* (liberation), first by withdrawing into the forest with his wife (*vanaprastha*), and then as a homeless ascetic (*sannyasi*). This ideal model has influenced the way old age is viewed, with a stress on detachment from worldly concerns in the later years.

Nowadays, within this framework, religious beliefs about God or the gods may vary enormously. A Hindu may follow one of three paths (*yoga* or *marga*) to salvation (*moksha* or *mukti*). The way of knowledge (Hindi *gyan*, Sanskrit *jnana*) follows the Upanishadic approach to mystical knowledge, and may include the psycho-physical discipline of yoga. The way of devotion (*bhakti*) focuses on a particular deity, most popularly Krishna, the avatar (incarnation) of Vishnu, or the mother goddess in one of her various forms. The popular sects, such as Swaminarayan, and The International Society of Krishna Consciousness (ISKCON or Hare Krishna), are devotional in nature,

2   'This term is virtually untranslatable. Generally it implies the idea of an eternally fixed and divine standard of conduct, a sacred law which is never to be altered, but only to be interpreted by legislation or by sound reform.' Basham (1977, p.244)
3   Twice born: boys from the three upper classes, who have access to a Sanskritic education, undergo an initiation at puberty (*upanayana*) in which they are invested with a sacred thread.

and the followers of Sathya Sai Baba worship him as a living deity. The third way, of action (*karma yoga*), was historically the way of sacrifice, but in the *Bhagavad Gita* and in the teachings of Mahatma Gandhi, the sacrifice is internalised to mean action without thought for its fruits, for example, without concern for the acquisition of good karma. Many Hindus describe their way of life as Sanatan Dharm, worshipping a variety of gods and performing their religious duties and sacrifices without belonging to a sect or following a specific path.

Bodily and spiritual harmony is maintained by careful attention to diet and appropriate exercise. Food is the stuff of the universe, and the right food contributes to both physical and spiritual well-being.[4] Ayurvedic medical treatment takes these into account in a holistic approach to health problems in a way few western medical doctors do, so that some Hindus who consult western doctors may also use traditional approaches.

The focus on the spiritual life enables one to approach death without anxiety, since it is merely a transition to the next life. This may be rebirth, often into the same family, or liberation, either understood as life in heaven with the god to whom one is devoted, or union with the absolute, Brahman. Some individuals have already achieved liberation in this life, so death is merely the shedding of the body. A good death is a conscious death entered willingly, having dealt with unfinished business and said goodbye to relatives and friends. In the *Bhagavad Gita*, Krishna says, 'And whoever, at the time of death, gives up his body and departs, thinking of Me alone, he comes to My status of being; of that there is no doubt' (*Bhagavad Gita* 8.5). The mind must be fixed on God, so it is necessary to know death is imminent, to perform an act of penance, and for relatives to be present to say farewell and help the dying person keep God in mind by chanting, singing hymns or reading from a favourite text, especially the *Bhagavad Gita* (Firth 1996, 1998).

Sikhism

Guru Nanak (1469–1539), the first of the ten Gurus who founded Sikhism, had a deep religious experience of one, loving and gracious God leading him

---

4   Matter (including food) is composed of three elements (*gunas*): light (*sattva*), energy (*rajas*), and heaviness (*tamas*), and someone who wishes to advance spiritually will choose appropriate *sattvik* foods, and avoid *tamsik* foods such as onions and garlic. There are also three humours which need to be harmoniously maintained by diet and religious and spiritual disciplines, and which contribute to the way a person ages. For a detailed discussion see Tilak (1989) pp.111ff.

to reject the temples, multiplicity of gods and the exclusive caste ranking of Hinduism, and the orthodoxy of politically dominant Islam, in favour of a simple devotionalism. God is without form or attributes, whose Word (*shabad*) is spoken through the Guru. Guru Nanak and his nine successors are seen as manifesting the same illuminating light or flame which now illuminates the sacred text, the *Guru Granth Sahib* (GGS). Sikhism is egalitarian, symbolised by the *langar*, the meal to which anyone is welcome. Women have an important religious role, leading services, preaching and reading the scriptures. Initiated (*Khalsa*) Sikhs wear the Five Ks: *kesh* (uncut hair), *kangha* (comb), *kirpan* (sword), *kara* (steel bracelet) and *kacch* (a pair of undershorts). They signify discipline, orderly spirituality, chastity, modesty and constraint. The *kara* also represents the unity of God, and the sword, readiness to fight in self-defence and in defence of the weak and unprotected. The daily life of the devout Sikh begins with bathing and morning prayer (*Japji* and *Swayyas*), and if possible further prayers should be said in the *gurdwara*. God should be kept in mind while at work, and prayers, *Rahiras* and *Kirtan Sohilla*, said at sunset and bedtime respectively.

Sikhs believe in transmigration generated by karma – attachment to the things of the material world leading to *maya*, the wrong point of view, and *haumai*, self-centredness. The individual has to depend entirely on God in obedience to His will (*hukam*), living a life of *sewa* (service) to God and to others, especially within the religious community, the *sangat* which according to Cole and Sambhi, 'is more than a brotherhood of like-minded people, it possesses mystical qualities' (1978, p.93; cf.68ff.). The true religious life, therefore, is that of the householder. Responsibility towards others is lifelong, but as physical strength wanes, activities change, and the *sewa* can be caring for and teaching grandchildren and receiving guests instead of the more demanding physical obligations. A model of old age is the third Guru, Amardas, who was Guru from the age of 73 until his death 22 years later in 1574. He was an imaginative and energetic reformer, especially regarding women, allowing widow remarriage, forbidding purdah and encouraging them to participate in the activities of the *gurdwara*. Another role model is Baba (Bhai) Buddha, the revered disciple of six of the ten Gurus, who lived for 125 years. It is assumed that age brings with it wisdom, and parents should be given great respect.

There are five stages of spiritual development, not associated with biological age, although it is assumed that age brings wisdom. These are piety, *Dharam Khand*; knowledge, *Gian Khand*; effort, *Saram Khand*; grace,

Karam Khand; and finally the stage or realm of truth, *Sach Khand*, which has to be experienced rather than described. Effort can only take one so far. In the last stages one has to depend upon God's grace: 'If man goes one step towards him The Lord comes a thousand towards man' (Cole and Sambhi 1978, p.80). The person who is 'God-minded' rather than self-centred, is '*gurmukh*', liberated from the bondage of self and worldly concerns, in a state of bliss and tranquillity known as '*sahaj*' (Cole and Sambhi 1978 pp.85–86). As a liberated person, s/he will not be reborn because s/he is already living in God's presence.

Sikhs should be ready for death, which 'does not wait for auspicious days or ask whether it is the light or dark side of the month' (GGS 1244). It is not to be feared or mourned for those who have been *gurmukh*, but rather celebrated. The person who is not prepared will suffer. Old age can be ugly, yet this ugliness is nothing to the ugliness of the spirit:

> His step has become ugly, his feet and hands slip, the skin of his body has shrivelled up. Eyes have become dim, ears deaf, but the self-centred man still does not know the Name. What have you gained by coming into this world, blind man? You have neither enshrined God in your heart or have you served the Guru. You are departing having lost even the accumulation of good works which you brought into the world. (GGS 1126)

Dying Sikhs wish to complete unfinished business, say farewells and have a final act of penance. Some Sikhs may wish to be laid on the floor,[5] and holy water, *amrit*, is placed in the mouth. It is important to focus the mind on God, so the evening prayer, *Kirtan Sohilla*, may be chanted, and the word, '*Waheguru*' (Wonderful Lord) said by the dying, if possible, and by those near him, at the point of death. A death in old age, in which the above aims are realised, is a good death. The family should be present to say goodbye and help the dying person. There are no priests, but the *granthi* (reader and *gurdwara* functionary) may attend if one is available (Cole and Sambhi (1978) pp.119–122; 177–178; Firth (1993) p.26ff; 254ff.; Kalsi (1996) p.30ff).

---

5   The *Rehat Maryada*, a guide to the Sikh way of life, forbids the placing of the body on the ground (Cole and Sambhi 1978, p.177), but as Kalsi shows (1996, p.32), this is still a common practice in some Sikh communities.

Islam

Like Sikhism, Islam does not institutionalise ageing, but recognises it as part of the process of life, which marks birth, the onset of puberty and marriage. According to the Qur'an:

> He it is God Who created you from dust, then from a drop (of seed) then from a clot, then brings you forth as a child, then (He lets you live) to attain full strength, then (He may let you live) to become shuyukh, (old people) – though some of you die before – and reach an appointed term. (40.67)

A Muslim is expected to continue in his/her ritual and social obligations as long as physical and mental health permit, in the life of a householder. This involves observing the Five Pillars: the declaration of faith (*Shahadah*), prayers five times a day (*Salat*), alms giving (*Zakat*), fasting (*Ramadan*), and at least once in a lifetime, the *Haj*, or pilgrimage to Makkah (Mecca). There is no conception of withdrawal, as in Hinduism, or asceticism apart from the discipline of fasting. According to Abdul-Rauf, the age of 60 or 70 is traditionally considered to be an average lifespan, although those failing in their fifties are considered elderly (1982, pp.175–6); Gardner (1996) found among Bengalis age was more to do with the stage of life cycle, usually becoming a grandparent. No one should be expected to exert him or herself beyond endurance. It is assumed that age brings with it wisdom and maturity which can be drawn on even when an individual is past physically demanding tasks. Whatever the mental and physical state of the individual, s/he should be treated with honour and respect, and cared for when in need:

> Whosoever does not treat our elders with respect and the young among us with sympathy is not worthy of being counted one among our members. A youth who has treated an elderly person with honour and respect for the sake of God, God shall cause people to treat him likewise in his old age. (cited in Abdul-Rauf 1982, p.79)

Special respect is reserved for parents, especially the mother, the Qur'an declaring:

> And your Lord has decreed that you should not worship (anything) save Him, and that you should treat the parents most kindly. If one of them or both attain old age with you, say not 'Fie' unto them nor repulse them, but speak to them in a noble way. And lower unto them the wing of humility through mercy: and pray: My Lord! Bestow Your mercy upon

them both, as they did care for me when I was a helpless little one. (17.23–24)

However, even parents can be mistaken, and if the offspring have to choose between obedience to God and to the parents, God must come first (29.8), continuing to treat them kindly and with respect.

Death is in God's hands and one should live in such a way that one is prepared at any time. God has promised resurrection into everlasting life to those who submit to Him, and His mercy and compassion give hope for forgiveness, although those who have sinned may be fearful of punishment in hell. Visiting the dying and the graves of the dead encourages awareness of death and discourages excessive attachment to material possessions. As death approaches, deficiencies in prayer and religious obligations should be remedied. Debts should be paid, and the dying person should make a will. S/he should forgive those who have been injured, and ask forgiveness, and also pray for God's forgiveness. The Qur'an, especially Chapter 36, Sura Ya-Sin, should be recited. At the point of death the person should say the *Kalima*, the profession of faith. Those around him/her have an obligation to assist in these last duties, placing him/her facing towards Makkah.[6] Muwahidi (1989) points out that there are no signs of good and bad deaths, as in Hinduism, mentioned in the Qur'an or the authentic sayings of the prophet, and while 'normally an honest person is expected to die a good death and a bad person is expected to have a painful and bad death, it could be otherwise' (p.45).

Asian Elders in Britain

Asian elders in Britain are proportionately smaller in numbers than their white British counterparts. They originate from very different geographical and linguistic areas with their own religious traditions – Hindu, Muslim and Sikh. Within each religion there are also considerable differences depending on sectarian affiliation, caste or class, education, economic status and migration history. Thus Bangladeshi, Pakistani and Gujarati Muslims not only speak different languages (in addition to the sacred language, Arabic) but belong to different sects and have their own local and family customs. Likewise, Hindus from, for example, Punjab and Gujarat may observe different festivals, eat different foods and belong to sects associated with

6   For detailed discussion, see Muwahidi (1989) p.38ff; Knappert (1989) p.55ff.

their own regions. Attitudes to ageing will be influenced not only by the above factors but also by their own biography, education, family organisation, housing and health, and their place in the local social and religious communities.

Apart from individuals settling in Britain, there have been several types of group migration. Men went to industrial areas in a process of chain migration, sending for relatives or friends as they settled. They lived in clusters, forming 'village-kin groups' sending money back to the subcontinent in the hope of returning one day (Desai 1963, p.15). Religious practice often lapsed until families began arriving, when efforts were made to organise places of worship.

From the late 1960s whole families came from East Africa as a result of Africanisation and Idi Amin's expulsions, with established religious traditions and strong links with the subcontinent reinforced by arranged marriages and education in Gujarat or the Punjab (Bhachu (1986), Michaelson (1987); Nye, (1995)). This led to religious conservatism and the maintenance of strong caste and linguistic bonds (Michaelson (1983) p.13ff; Burghart (1987) p.7ff). Hindus and Sikhs also came from India, Muslims from Mirpur in Pakistan and Sylhet in Bangladesh, and smaller numbers from Fiji, Mauritius and the West Indies. The tendency to settle in clusters has led to different linguistic, religious, class and caste groupings in different British cities. There are currently about 1,431,348 South Asians from India, Pakistan and Bangladesh in Britain, 35 per cent of whom were born in this country.[7]

As families settled, mosques, *gurdwaras* and temples were built, and the 'myth of return' faded (Anwar 1979, Gardner 1997). A growing number of elders are those who worked in Britain and have retired here, and they are reluctant to return to the homeland because of children settled in Britain. However, many Muslims wish to be buried in their homeland, so that they can be assured of the traditional burial,[8] have the prayers for the soul and be

---

7   In Britain there are approximately 823,821 Indians, 449,646 Pakistanis and 157,881
     Bangladeshis (OPCS Census Report 1991 cited in Ballard 1994, p.7). Approximately
     half the Indians are Hindus and half are Sikhs. About 70 per cent of the Hindu
     population is ethnically Gujarati, 15 per cent Punjabi, and the remainder are mainly
     from Uttar Pradesh, Bengal, South Indian provinces and Maharashtra.

8   There is a discrepancy between the requirement to bury immediately where the person
     has died, and the prohibition of post-mortems, and the desire to send the body back to
     India, Pakistan or Bangladesh, requiring embalming, which would injure the dead as
     much as a post-mortem.

visited by kin (Gardner 1996). Many Hindus and Sikhs want their ashes returned to Indian rivers.

The belief that Asians care for their own has created problems of adequate service provision (Gardner 1997). Sometimes the communities resist recognising problems of unwanted elders, since this destroys the myth of the caring joint family. Council housing and inner-city terraces or flats are inappropriate for extended families, who are sometimes forcibly split up. While it is usual in the subcontinent for parents to live with their sons, in Britain daughters sometimes take responsibility for elderly parents. There are reports of 'granny dumping'. Tahira Mohammed of Newham Age Concern reports that there are around 40 'dumped' Asians every week (Daly 1997). Various schemes have been established all over the country providing housing and women's refuges for Asian elders and abused women.[9] Neeta Josi, at the British Asian Women's Association suggests that about 700 individuals a year need rehousing, usually because they have been rejected by sons and daughters-in-law. Mina Patel, of Age Concern UK, puts this down to the intense economic and social pressures Asian families are exposed to: 'Older people are not respected like they were back home. There has been a big shift in the balance which now favours the bread-winner, as youngsters take on more and more Western values' (Daly 1997).

Elders left at home while the sons and daughters-in-law work may be lonely and isolated if they are located some distance from the mosque, *gurdwara* or temple (Blakemore and Boneham 1994, p.80). If they do not speak or read English they may be afraid to go out, unable to read signs or ask directions. An elderly Hindu *sannyasi* was invited to live with his sister's family in the hope that he would act as temple pandit, but he returned to India because he could not tolerate the cold which forced him to stay indoors, problems of mobility and the lack of access to religious facilities. Women are even more vulnerable if they live outside the community and have transport problems. There may also be serious misunderstandings with their Anglicised children or grandchildren, who may be, or appear to be, rejecting the traditional beliefs and customs.

When Amarjit Kaur, a Sikh woman, 84, came to live with her son Jaswant, his wife, Karanjit, (pseudonyms) and their son and his wife, she found it

<hr>

9   For examples, see *Age and Race: Double discrimination: Life in Britain Today for Ethnic Minority Elders, 1995,* Commission for Racial Equality and Age Concern; Eastwards trust Annual Report, 1997, Newham, Southampton is also making provision for elderly Asians.

difficult to understand the need of the women to work outside the house, and the family habit of having conferences to make joint decisions. She could not get to the *gurdwara* unless she was taken there, and the family rearranged their work schedules so that someone would always be with her at home. Although some of her grandchildren did not speak Punjabi, she tried to establish an affectionate relationship based on friendly hugs and touch. A Sikh doctor observed:

> Many people feel, 'Now we are wealthy, let's bring the old folks here.' It is making a mistake because the elderly are sad and lonely, uprooted from the familiar environment where they had a role to play and a sense of continuity. There they were useful and accepted, with a full day. Here they are lost and lonely, and the [younger] women work whereas there they did not.

Those who live with easy access to other members of their community and their places of worship may find satisfaction from communal prayers and activities and often become more active in the life of the community as they become older. Mr Gaurang, a Gujarati Hindu from Tanzania, retired early to care for a sick wife, receiving little support from the Hindu community. He thinks that only about 1 per cent of British Hindus withdraw and has himself remained active. A follower of Sanatan Dharm, he sees God as Rama and Krishna, but believes one can learn from all religions, which teach the same things about being honest and kind. He prays for ten minutes every morning and fifteen minutes at night. He often chants, and reads various religious books such as the *Mahabharata*, the *Bhagavata Purana* and the *Bhagavad Gita*, 'which keeps you calm and steady'.

Mr Yusuf, a Sunni Muslim,[10] also has to care for a sick wife. He came to Britain in 1963 for further education, leaving his wife and family in Swat. Since 1987 she has visited Britain for periods of two or three years because he was alone, but returned to Pakistan to be with her family. She is currently in Britain for medical treatment, but as soon as she is well enough she wishes to return. She only speaks Pushtu so her range of contacts is limited to other Pathans. She is lonely and misses her family, but refuses to go out, spending most of her time praying. Yusuf is critical of the emphasis on drugs in Britain.

10   Sunni Muslims are followers of the Sunna (practice) of the majority Community. Shi'a
      maintain that the legitimacy of the leadership of Islam after the prophet's death lay in
      his cousin and son-in-law Ali and Ali's descendants. Ali had 'the guidance of heaven',
      which still lies in his descendents, the Imams (Basham 1971, p.170).

In Swat, when Yusuf was studying physics, a doctor said that 10 per cent of the treatment was by the doctor and 90 per cent by Allah: 'When Allah pleases, water will be your medicine'. Yusuf is involved in the local Muslim community, and is passionately committed to furthering the dissemination of Islam. He is distressed by the way westerners react against Islam and label it 'fundamentalist':

> We still believe the Bible as the Holy Book of its time, from the sky, from Allah, but now Allah says you must believe in me and my prophets, and Mohammed, peace be upon him, is his prophet for this time. He has given this message to the nations. Why don't you recognise this and become a Muslim?

Religious Experience

A number of informants spoke of the depth of their devotion and love of God, as well as the way they have tried to come to terms with suffering. A Punjabi widow, Mrs Tandon, said,

> If you are too attached, death is very painful because you know you have to leave everybody and everything behind, whereas if you start giving up things you find a different kind of happiness. You realise the fact that your family and friends are not really what you think they are, they are individual souls, so the stronger the attachment the more intense the pain. (Firth 1996, p.98)

Mrs Tandon, 70, came to Britain in 1968 from Kenya with her family, and was widowed in 1985. A devout member of Arya Samaj,[11] she lives alone, and is unable to get to the temple unless she has transport. She thinks religious life is difficult for householders, but is increasingly aware of God's involvement in the world. Life is 'sukh-dukh', happiness and sadness together, so that sometimes one is sick or short of money. Happiness is a gift, or the result of good karma, not a right. God set karma in motion, and ultimately death is in God's hands, so there is no point fighting it. Speaking shortly after her son's death, she said:

---

11 Arya Samaj: a Hindu reform movement founded in the nineteenth century by Swami Dayanand Saraswati. He rejected Brahmin domination, use of images and the emphasis on purity and pollution, wishing to return to the purity of the Vedic teachings. The main focus of worship is the Vedic fire ritual, the havan. It is particularly popular among Panjabis.

If you are a *bhakta* (devotee), then everything that comes to you, you accept, as God's *iccha* (wish). If He wants to take your son or your husband, what can you do? If you believe in God then you have to recognise everything comes from God, He is powerful over us all. After birth is death, everyone dies. God gives us a body and *atma* (soul), and when the body is dead and burned the atma remains eternal. Once you know this, why do you want to fight or be angry? Who is dead? Nobody is dead if you believe the *atma* (soul) is eternal. People come and go, come and go, and you think, my parents have died, others have died, then [the people who come to visit] say, 'My son has died, my daughter has died', and share with you. In every house death has come. When I cried, I reminded myself of this and then I had *shanti*, peace.

Although we have free will God is in overall control of events, intervening to assist people through others: 'God sends people when you suffer. He hasn't got *rup* (a form) like you, only *shakti*, (strength), and He comes into people and gets them to go and help others. I can't go out when I am in *dukh* (sorrow), and people like you come and offer to help.'

She spends an hour a day in her devotions. She uses a *mala* (rosary) of 108 beads, saying the *Gayatri Mantra*[12] with each one, and says Sai Baba's universal prayer for all faiths: 'If we pray to You, You bless everyone. Everything is in You. We are blessed by You, and then we bless younger people.'

Mr and Mrs Krishnan (a pseudonym), Panjabi Brahmins, came to Britain from India in 1967. After years of vigorous activity in the local temple, they learned about Sathya Sai Baba at a time that Mrs Krishnan developed heart problems. Mr Krishnan had started to believe even before they went to see him: 'We wanted to go, but waited for Him to call us, we surrendered to Him'. In a miraculous fashion they obtained visas and leave from their work and went to India. 'He was full of love, I could feel His rays. He took me under His guidance. From that moment my life changed.' This sense of being in God's presence and care saw them through the most difficult year of their lives, as Mrs Krishnan had to undergo major heart surgery on the same day that Mr Krishnan received his redundancy notice. They now have monthly meetings in their home when English and Indian followers sing hymns, discuss Baba's

12   *Gayatri Mantra*: 'Let us think on the lovely splendour of the god Savitra, that he may inspire our minds' (*Rig Veda* III.62.10; Basham 1971, p.165). This sacred mantra is used in all important rituals.

teachings, and pray. There is a Sai Baba shrine in their living room and devotion to him is the focus of their lives. They are both active in local interfaith activities and in the temple, and Mr Krishnan says that he wants to remain active until the end of his life, while developing an inner detachment:

> My view is that I still have obligations to fulfil as long as my limbs, my wisdom, my skill is still working rather than sitting in one place praying. This is my view of sannyas; rather than living life alone like a log I'm doing my karma right to the end – karma yoga – service, and bhakti – He gives me His strength and love and I pass this on to the community.

God's continuous presence in daily life, and his love and support in the face of suffering has been the experience of Kailash Gopal Singh Puri, a Sikh, now in her seventies. Her childhood in a religious family in Rawalpindi gave her a model of faith and devotion, which carried them through the trauma of Partition, and has helped her throughout her life. She cannot be grateful enough to God, because she can never repay his gifts: 'Without religion I would have been like a tree with dried roots, without any strength or power to sustain hot, cold, snow storms, and would have fallen down'. A Punjabi folk proverb says, 'When you are young you look after cattle, then you start farming and bring up the family. When you are old you have a *mala* (rosary) in your hand; you are giving God gratitude for the life He gave you.' It is only in the context of the full life of the householder that one can give due place to God in worship, devotion and service. Kailash Puri is a lecturer, has been an agony aunt on several Punjabi papers and has written 31 books, including an autobiography called, in Panjabi, *I am Grateful Millions of Times.* Her husband, Dr Gopal Singh Puri, an eminent scientist, encouraged her to develop her own skills and talents, and they ran a yoga centre together for 21 years. Her faith has helped her cope with his death, and she feels his presence all the time and sees him in her dreams: 'He knows how forlorn I am, he is watching, and when I leave this earth he will take me. I have vivid pictures of where we will go. He always says we have come for seven reincarnations and will never be parted.' She has incredible visions and revelations: 'I have amazing experiences of the radiance of the nature of mind, luminosity or the clear light which manifests as sound, colour and light'. Kailash wishes to die writing, meditating, loving and blessing her children, and to absorb herself in worship and grateful prayers.

Many immigrants have experienced multiple losses, especially those who were forcibly moved, such as some from East Africa, and those who have lived through Partition, whether Muslim, Sikh or Hindu. The granddaughter of Maharajah Balbir Singh of Faridkot, Rupinder Kaur Mann, 75, moved to Lahore on her marriage, but she and her husband lost everything at Partition, returning to India as refugees. Rebuilding their lives, she worked as a social worker and was a member of the Panjab Parliament for 15 years. When her husband died seven years ago, she came to Britain to live with her younger daughter. Rupinder Kaur has turned more and more to religion, spending much of her time in her room praying. She is fascinated by other religious traditions, and has had visions, including one of Mohammed, one of Guru Gobind Singh, the tenth Guru, pulling her out of a river, and one of Jesus Christ wearing a cream woollen outfit, his face half hidden by a shawl, and his hand upraised. He smiled at her. 'I felt He was holding me, I felt so close – *bilkul shakti* (lots of power).' She had a vision of Shiva, in which she was told that although her life was finished, her son's prayers at Gwalior had extended it. She saw what she thought was the record of her past life, but was told that it was not yet time to open it. She now prays daily for her son to give him back the years he offered her. When she prays she sees a beautiful light golden eye, which she believes is God's eye, and often sees beautiful glowing green grapes. The prayer, the *Mul Mantra*,[13] runs through her mind all the time, even when she is in conversation. She also repeats *Waheguru* as often as she can, on each breath. 'Just talking about God makes him present and he teaches us how to pray.'

Community and Interfaith

Several informants including Kailash Gopal Singh Puri, Charanjit Ajit Singh and Mr Krishnan (above) felt committed to furthering an understanding of their faith within their own communities, particularly in helping the young to explore their identity and find ways of being better Hindus, Muslims and Sikhs in British secular society. They were also committed to dialogue with other faiths. During his years as a teacher Mr Mohammed Ryami (a pseudonym), originally from Zanzibar, was involved in teaching about Islam, especially to teachers, and was, and still is, committed to interfaith activities. On retiring he is busier than ever within the Muslim community, on committees concerned with ethnic minorities, and helping individuals and

---

13 *Mul Mantra*: 'This Being is One; the Truth; immanent in all things; sustainer of all things; creator of all things. Immanent in creation. Without fear and without enmity. Not subject to time. Beyond birth and death. Self manifesting. Known by the Guru's grace.' According to Cole this mantra is 'regarded as the essence of Sikh theology', with 'pride of place in the Guru Granth Sahib' (Cole 1990, p.111).

families in trouble. He is concerned with issues of Muslim identity, especially for the young, as even westernised Muslims are rejected. He sees the older generation developing a new conservatism towards the young, forgetting that they might once have danced and worn western dress. Young women are being encouraged to wear the *hijab*, the headscarf. He feels the need to get back to his own Islamic roots and society, which he had lost touch with when he was younger, aware of 'the reward of heaven to come'. He would feel comfortable ageing in Africa where care does not devolve on one person and there is a sense of family and community, but his wife has ties in Britain. He is glad to be able to say prayers at the appropriate time, and go to the mosque each Friday. He has not yet managed to go on the Haj, the pilgrimage to Makkah, and longs for the opportunity 'to begin with a clean slate'.

For Bashir Rahim retirement has meant serving and teaching the local Muslim community and engagement in interfaith dialogue and worship. Age brings experience, and there is an obligation to pass that on. A former diplomat and Islamic scholar, he turned down an opportunity to work for the Commonwealth Secretariat and retired to Fareham to act as Imam to the local Shi'a community. Like Mr Ryami, his concern is to find ways of being a good British Muslim. The young, highly Anglicised community are in danger of losing their Islamic tradition to pop culture, but there have to be ways of being better Muslims without separation and isolation. Elders want to replicate the life and atmosphere of the old country, but if children and young people are going to be interested, it is necessary to adapt, cutting out some of the rituals and encouraging talking and dialogue. At the Shi'a centre in Wickham there is a weekly exegesis and discussion open to both men and women, to which Christians are welcome. At the Saturday school Mr Rahim talks to the children, stressing their duty to acquire knowledge, as they have to be better than the best of their white peers. His wife, Sugra, helps lead the women, who meet monthly to discuss ethical issues from a religious perspective, but it also provides an opportunity to socialise. Interfaith activities demand that each community examines itself honestly and understands its own beliefs and traditions, as well as developing openness and tolerance, which might also help the churches with their problems with secularisation and apathy. The Bishop of Portsmouth is an enthusiastic ally, and they share in services, such as celebrating the birth of Jesus and the birth of the Prophet Mohammed's grandson. Exclusivity helps neither community: 'The good people, the ones who are liked by God, always have an opportunity of showing their love to their loved ones: that in itself is a testimony of how they are loved by God'.

Conclusion

Asian elders in Britain, it is clear, are not a homogeneous group. There are some who are marginalised because of poverty, poor housing and ill health, racism, and, for a minority, exclusion by their own families. Prayer may be a natural solace, but without mobility, shared worship may be impossible. Two of the widows interviewed for this chapter spent more time in reading, meditation and prayer partly because they were isolated from the Hindu temple and the Sikh *gurdwara*. Service provision for Asian elders may be poor because it is assumed that they will be cared for within their own communities, although Asian housing organisations are springing up in many cities. Those with education, resources and a family and social support system have opportunities to serve the community on committees, teaching and, for some, engagement with other faiths. Religion is not a part-time activity but a way of life, set in the context of a living belief in the divine, the importance of the scriptures as authoritative guides, and life after death which demands preparation and readiness at all times.

Acknowledgements

My gratitude to Charanjit Ajit Singh for information about the Gurus and texts, Tahira Mohammed of Age Concern, Daljit Singh Grewal, Rupinder Kaur Mann, 'Mr Gaurang', Bashir and Sugra Rahim, 'Mr and Mrs Krishnan', Mohammed Ryami, Kailash Gopal Singh Puri, Shafquat Shah, Aurin Sood, 'Mrs Tandon', and Mr Yusuf, for their openness and generosity, Katie Gardner, and Eleanor Nesbitt for reading and commenting on the script.

References

Abdalati, H. (1975) *Islam in Focus*. Indianapolis: American Trust Publications.

Abdul-Rauf, M. (1982) 'The ageing in Islam.' In F. Tiso (ed) (1982) *Aging: Spiritual Perspectives*. Lakeworth: Sunday Publications Inc.

Age Concern and the Commission for Racial Equality (1997) *Age and Race: Double Discrimination. Life in Britain Today for Ethnic Minority Elders*. London: Age Concern and CRE.

Anwar, M. (1979) *The Myth of Return: Pakistanis in Britain*. London: Heineman.

Autton, N. (1969) *The Pastoral Care of the Mentally Ill*. London: SPCK Library of Pastoral Care Series.

Baldock, J. and Ungerson, C. (1994) *Becoming Consumers of Community Care*. York: Joseph Rowntree Foundation.

Ballard, R. (ed) (1994) *Desh Pardesh: The South Asian Presence in Britain*. London: Hurst.

Baltes, M. and Baltes, P. (1986) *Psychology of Control and Ageing*. Hillside, New Jersey: Lawrence Erlbaum.

Baltes, P. and Reese, H. (1982) 'The lifespan perspective in developmental psychology.' M. Boornstein and M. Lamb (eds) *Aging and Cognitive Processes*. New York: Plenum.

Bancroft, A. (1989) *Weavers of Wisdom: Women Mystics of the Twentieth Century*. London: Penguin Arkana.

Barnado's (1993) *Release*. 20 November. Ilford.

Barot, R. (ed) (1993) *Religion and Ethnicity: Minorities and Social Change in the Metropolis*. Kampen: Kok Pharos.

Basham, A.L. (1971) *The Wonder that was India*. London: Fontana Collins.

Basham, A.L. (1977) 'Hinduism.' In R.C. Zaehner (1977) *The Concise Encyclopaedia of Living Faiths*. London: Hutchinson.

Bell, J. and McGregor, I. (1995) 'A challenge to stage theories of dementia.' In T. Kitwood and S. Benson (eds) *The New Culture of Dementia Care*. London: Hawker Publications.

Berger, A. *et al.* (eds) (1989) *Perspectives on Death and Dying: Cross-Cultural and Multi-disciplinary Views*. Philadelphia: Charles Press.

Berger, P. (1969) *A Rumour of Angels*. London: Penguin Books.

Berggren-Thomas, P. and Griggs, M. (1995) 'Spirituality in aging: spiritual need or spiritual journey?' *Journal of Gerontological Nursing 21*, 3, 6–9.

Bhachu, P. (1985) *Twice Migrants: East African Sikh Settlers in Britain.* London: Tavistock Press.

Bhagavad Gita (1948) translated by Sarvapalli Radhakrishnan. New York: Harper and Bros.

Blakemore, K. and Boneham, M. (1994) *Age, Race and Ethnicity.* Buckingham: Open University Press.

Bonhoeffer, P. (1953) *Letters and Papers from Prison.* SCM.

Bowker, J. (1991) *The Meanings of Death.* Cambridge University Press.

Buckland, S. (1995) 'Well-being, Personality and Residential Care.' In T. Kilwood and S. Basm, *The New Culture of Dementia Care.* London: Walker Publications.

Burghart, R. (ed) (1987) *Hinduism in Great Britain: The Perpetuation of Religion in an Alien Cultural Milieu.* London: Tavistock.

Campbell, A. (1985) *Paid to Care.* London: SPCK.

Cassidy, S. (1988) *Sharing the Darkness: The Spirituality of Caring.* London: Darton, Longman and Todd.

de Chardin, T. (1957) *Le Milieu Divin.* London: Collins.

The Christian Education Movement (1997) *Looking Inwards, Looking Outwards: Exploring Life's Possibilities. Teacher Handbook and Student Resource.* Derby: The Christian Education Movement, sponsored by the John Templeton Foundation.

Church of England Board of Social Responsibility (1990) *Ageing.* London: Church House Publicity.

Cnaan, R. (1997) *Social and Community Involvement of Religious Congregations.* Philadelphia School of Social Work, University of Pennsylvania.

Cole, W. and Sambhi, P. (1978) *The Sikhs, Their Religious Beliefs and Practices.* London: Routledge and Kegan Paul.

Cole, W. (1990) *A Popular Dictionary of Sikhism.* London: Curzon Press.

Coles, R. (1992) *The Spiritual Life of Children.* London: Harper Collins.

Cox, H. (1965) *The Secular City.* New York: Macmillan.

Daly, M. (1997) *The Big Issue,* 26 May–1 June No. 234.

Davies, P. (1992) *The Mind of God.* London: Penguin Books.

Department of Health (1991) *Practitioners and Managers Guide to Care Management and Assessment.* London: HMSO.

Desai, R. (1963) *Indian Immigrants in Britain.* London: Oxford University Press.

Dickenson, D. and Johnson, M. (eds) (1993) *Death and Dying.* London: Sage.

Duncan, D. (1988) *Health and Healing: A Ministry to Wholeness.* Edinburgh: The Saint Andrew Press.

Eastwards Trust (1997) *Annual Report: Age and Race: Double Discrimination: Life in Britain Today for Ethnic Minority Elders, 1995.* Commission for Racial Equality and Age Concern: Newham.

Elliott, C. (1995) *Memory and Salvation.* London: DLT.

Eliot, T.S. (1963) *Collected Poems 1909–1962.* London: Faber and Faber.

Ellor, Rev J. (1997) 'Spiritual well-being defined.' In *Spirituality and Ageing* (1 July). The San Francisco Ministry to Nursing Homes, 1775 Clay Street, San Francisco, CA 94109.

Erikson, E. (1963) *Childhood and Society*. Second Edition. New York: W. Norton and Company.

Firth, S. (1993) 'Approaches to death in Hindu and Sikh communities in Britain.' In D. Dickenson and M. Johnson (eds) (1993) *Death and Dying*. London :Sage.

Firth, S. (1996) 'The good death: attitudes of British Hindus.' In P. Jupp and G. Howarth (eds) (1996) *Contemporary Issues in the Sociology of Death, Dying and Disposal*. Basingstoke: Macmillan.

Firth, S. (1997) *Dying, Death and Bereavement in a British Hindu Community*. Leuven: Peeters.

Fischer, K. (1988) *Women at the Well: Feminist Perspectives on Spiritual Direction*. London: SPCK.

Fischer, K. (1996) *Moving On*. London: SPCK.

Froggatt, A. and Shamy, E. (1992) *Dementia: A Christian Perspective*. London: Christian Council on Ageing Occasional Paper Number 5.

Froggatt, A. and Shamy, E. (1992) *Dementia: A Christian Perspective*. Christian Council on Ageing Occasional Paper No. 5.

Gardner, K. (1996) 'Death and burial amongst Bengali Muslims in Tower Hamlets, East London.' Paper given at the conference, 'A Comparative Study of the South Asian Diaspora Religious Experience in Britain, Canada and USA'. School of Oriental and African Studies, November.

Gardner, K. (1997) 'Ageing, poverty and exclusion amongst Bengali elders in Tower Hamlets.' London, report submitted to Age Concern.

The Guardian (1997) 'Tale of the century.' 17 November, p.8.

Goldsmith, M. (1996) *Hearing the Voice of People with Dementia*. London: Jessica Kingsley Publishers.

Harpur, T. (1991) *Life after Death*. Toronto: McClelland and Stewart.

Harrelson, W. (1980) *The Ten Commandments and Human Rights*. Philadelphia: Fortress.

Harris, M. (1991) *Dance of the Spirit: The Seven Steps of Women's Spirituality*. New York and London: Bantham Books.

Heschel, Rabbi A.J. (1973) 'Nachdichtung' from *Der Shen Haus 'foresh Mentsch*. Self-published.

Hira, B. (1997) 'Migration, culture and social change: an intergenerational experience of Indians, Pakistanis and Bangladeshis.' Dissertation submitted for MSc. in Ethnic Relations, Department of Sociology, University of Bristol.

Howatch, S. (1997) *A Question of Integrity*. London: Little, Brown and Company.

Hugo, V. 'Booz Endorum'. *Oxford Book of French Verse*. Oxford: OUP.

Iona Community. (1989) *Worship Book*. Glasgow: Wild Goose Publications.

John Mananzan, M. (ed) (1992) *Women and Religion: A collection of Essays, Personal Histories and Contextualised Liturgies.* Manila: The Institute of Women's Studies, St Scholastica's College.

John Mananzan, M. *et al.* (1996) *Women Resisting Violence: Spirituality for Life.* Maryknoll, New York: Orbis Books.

Jupp, P. and Howarth, G. (eds) (1996) *Contemporary Issues in the Sociology of Death, Dying and Disposal.* London: Macmillan.

Kalsi, S. (1996) 'Change and continuity in the funeral rituals of Sikhs in Britain.' In *op. cit.* P. Jupp and G. Howarth (eds) pp.30–43.

King, U. (1993) *Women and Spirituality: Voices of Protest and Promise.* Second edition. London: Macmillan.

Kitwood, T. and Bredin, K. (1992) *Person to Person.* Essex: Gale Centre Publications.

Kitwood, T. and Benson, S. (1995) *The New Culture of Dementia Care.* London: Hawkes Publications.

Knappert, J. (1989) 'The concept of death and the afterlife in Islam.' In A. Berger *et al.* (eds) (1989) *Perspectives of Death and Dying.* Philadelphia: Charles Press.

Knott, K. (1986) *Hinduism in Leeds.* Leeds University (Community Religions Project).

Kung, H. (1980) *Does God Exist?* London: Collins.

Kung, H. (1982) *Eternal Life.* London: SCM Press.

Loyola, I. *The Spiritual Exercises of St Ignatius* [tr. L.J. Puhl] Chicago: Loyola University Press.

Meier, J. (1980) *Matthew.* Dublin: Veritas.

Methodist Conference Commission on Worship (1988) *Let the People Worship.* Peterborough: Methodist Publishing House.

Michaelson, M. (1983) 'Caste, kinship and marriage: a study of two Gujurati trading castes in England.' Unpublished PhD thesis, University of London.

Michaelson, M. (1987) 'Domestic Hinduism in a Gujarati trading caste.' In R. Burghart (ed) (1987) *Hinduism in Great Britain.* London: Tavistock.

Murphy, C. (1994) *Life Story Work and People with Dementia.* Stirling: Dementia Services Development Centre.

Muwahidi, A.A. (1989) 'Islamic perspectives on death and dying.' In A. Berger *et al.* (eds) (1989) *Perspectives on Death and Dying.* Philadelphia: Charles Press.

Nelson, D., Bennett, D. and Xu, J. (1997) 'Recollective and automatic uses of memory.' In *Journal of Experimental Psychology: Learning Memory and Cognition 23,* 872–885.

Nouwen, H. (1994) *Our Greatest Gift.* London: Hodder and Stoughton.

Nuland, S. (1994) *How We Die.* London: Chatto & Windus.

Nye, A. (1995) *A Peace for our Gods: The Construction of an Edinburgh Hindu Temple Community.* London: Curzon Press.

OPCS Census Report (1991). London: HMSO.

Osborne, C. (1993) *The Reminiscence Handbook*. London: Age Exchange.

The Oxford Companion to the Mind. Oxford: OUP.

Pailin, D. (1986) *Groundwork of Philosophy of Religion*. London: Epworth Press Ltd.

Pascal, B. (1966) *Pensées*. Introduction and Translation, A.J. Krailsheimer. London: Penguin Books.

Perham, M. (1984) *Liturgy Pastoral and Parochial*. London: SPCK.

Polkinghorne, J. (1994) *Science and Christian Belief*. London: SPCK.

Puri, K. (1986) *Bar Juon Lakh Beria* [*I'm Grateful Millions of Times*] New Delhi: Naugaj Publishers.

Quaker Faith and Practice (1995) London: Religious Society of Friends.

Reid, C. (1968) *Malcolm Sargent*. London: Hodder and Stoughton.

Rig Veda, The (1980) translated by Wendy O'Flaherty. Harmondsworth: Penguin.

Sacks, O. (1982) *Awakenings*. London: Picador.

Schachter-Shalomi, Z. and Miller, R. (1995) *From Age-ing to Sage-ing*. New York: Warner Books Inc.

Schweitzer, P. (1993) *Age Exchanges: Reminiscence for Children and Older People*. London: Age Exchange.

Simkins, Dr J. (1995) *Leading Services in Residential Homes*. Peterborough: Methodist Publishing House.

Stevenson, K. (1981) *Symbolism and the Liturgy*. Grove Liturgical Study No.26. Nottingham: Grove Books Ltd.

Storr, A. (1986) *Jung*. London: Fontana Modern Masters.

Stuart-Hamilton, I. (1994) *The Psychology of Ageing*. London: Jessica Kingsley Publishers.

Thirteen Principle Upanishads, (1983) translated by R.E. Hume. London: Oxford University Press.

Thiselton, A. (1986) *Language Liturgy and Meaning*. Grove Liturgical Study No.2 Nottingham: Grove Books Ltd.

Tilak, K.S. (1989) *Religion and Aging in the Indian Tradition*. New York: State University.

Tiso, F.V. (1982) (ed) *Aging: Spiritual Perspectives*. Lake Worth: Sunday Publications, Inc.

Treetops, J. (1992) *A Daisy Among the Dandelions: The Church's Ministry with Older People*. Leeds: Leeds Faith in Elderly People (Leeds Church Institute, Leeming House, Vicar Lane, Leeds LS2 7JF).

Treetops, J. (1996) *Holy, Holy, Holy: The Church's Ministry with People with Dementia*. Leeds: Leeds Faith in Elderly People.

Underhill, E. (1993) *The Spiritual Life: Great Spiritual Truths for Everyday Life*. Oxford: Oneworld.

Vanstone, W. (1982) *The Stature of Waiting*. London: Darton Longman and Todd.

Vonnegut, K. (1963) *Cat's Cradle*. New York: Bantam Doubleday Dell.

Warren, R. (1995) *Building Missionary Congregations.* London: Church House Publishing.

Waterhouse, E.S. (1947) *The Philosophical Approach to Religion.* Peterborough: Epworth.

Weaver, G. (1986) 'Senile dementia and resurrection theology.' *Theology Today* 42, 4, 444–456.

Weldon, M. and Bellinger, K. (1997) 'Collective memory: collaborative and individual processes in remembering.' *Journal of Experimental Psychology: Learning Memory and Cognition 23*, 1160–1175.

Wilce, H. (1996) 'Age No Concern'. *Times Educational Supplement.* 23 January.

Wolff, H.W. (1974) *The Anthropology of the Old Testament.* London: SCM.

Working Party Report on 'Spirituality' (1977) Dunblane: Scottish Churches House.

Yearly Meeting of the Religious Society of Friends (Quakers) in Britain (1994) *Quaker Faith and Practice: The Book of Christian Discipline of the Yearly Meeting of the Religious Society of Friends (Quakers) in Britain.* London.

Zaehner, R.C. (1977) *The Concise Encyclopaedia of Living Faiths.* London: Hutchinson.

The Contributors

Mary Austin is a Methodist minister currently in the Bloxwich and Willenhall Circuit. At the time of writing she was a minister in local appointment in Maidenhead and part-time chaplain for the East Berkshire Community Health Trust at St Mark's Hospital.

James A. Crampsey is the Provincial Superior of the Society of Jesus.

Shirley Firth, a quaker, is a freelance writer and lecturer on mulitcultural aspects of death and bereavement, and author of *Dying, Death and Bereavement in a British Hindu Community.*

Malcolm Goldsmith is the Rector of St Cuthbert's Episcopal Church in Colinton, Edinburgh, and associated with the Dementia Services Development Centre at the University of Stirling where he was formerly a Research Fellow. He is the author of *Hearing the Voice of Older People with Dementia*, published by Jessica Kingsley.

Margaret Goodall is a minister in the Milton Keynes circuit of the Methodist Church and chaplain of Westbury, Methodist Homes for the Aged, for those with dementia.

Jenny Goodman is a medical doctor, psychotherapist and writer on medical ethics.

Jeffrey W. Harris is retired Secretary of the Methodist Home Mission Division.

Gerard W. Hughes is an international writer and teacher on Ignatian spirituality. He is the author of *God of Surprises.*

Albert Jewell is Pastoral Director of Methodist Homes for the Aged.

Ursula King is Professor of Theology and Religious Studies at the University of Bristol.

Helen Oppenheimer Oxon. M.A., B.Phil; Lambeth D.D., is a writer on Christian ethics.

Phyllida Parsloe is Emeritus Professor of Social Work, University of Bristol.

Rabbi Zalman Schachter-Shalomi holds the World Wisdom Chair at the Nargea Institute in Boulder, Colorado. In 1989 he founded the Spiritual Eldering Institute. He is the co-author with Roald Miller of *From Ageing to Sageing: A Profound New Vision of Growing Older.*

Muriel Bishop Summers is a member of the Religious Society of Friends (Quakers) and co-facilitator of 'The Time of Your Life' workshops for women and men over 65 under the auspices of Woodbrooke College in Birmingham. She was previously the Director of Project Reconciliation, an outreach ministry to prisoners and ex-prisoners, a project of the First Baptist Church, Kingston, Ontario, Canada.

Metropolitan Anthony of Sourozh is a member of the Russian Orthodox Patriarchal Church.

Jackie Treetops is an Anglican priest and author of titles on the Church's ministry to older people and people with dementia.

Penelope Wilcock is a former hospice chaplain and author of *Spiritual Care of Dying and Bereaved People.*

Paul H. Wilson B.A., (Liverpool), B.D., M.Phil. (Manchester), is a Methodist minister, hospital chaplain and member of the Christian Council on Ageing, Dementia Working Group.

Subject Index

Author Index